Castellón, Valer

valencian
gastronomy and cuisine

Photography Oriol Aleu
Cuisine and style Ana Torróntegui
Texts and recipes Toni Monné
Graphic design Joseta Torróntegui

TRIANGLE▼BOOKS

valencian_cuisine

© 2014, Triangle Postals S.L.,
Pere Tudurí, 8
07710 Sant Lluís, Menorca

Coordination and editing of project: Oriol Aleu
Cuisine and style: Ana Torróntegui
Cooking assistant: Alexandra Torres
Texts and recipes: Toni Monné
Graphic design and layout: Joseta Torróntegui
Photography: Oriol Aleu
Translation: Steve Cedar

© 2014, Toni Monné for the texts
© 2014, Oriol Aleu for the photos
© 2014, Oriol Casanovas for the photos: pages 62, 63(2), 69(3)

It is prohibited, without the written authorisation of the copyright holders to reproduce this work partially or totally by any means or process, including reprography and computerised treatment, and the distribution of copies of it by means of hiring or public loan. Printed in Spain

ISBN: 978-84-84478-589-7
Legal registration: DL:Me-265-2013

Printed in Barcelona
Printed by: C. Estelar, 2017

Introduction	05
The landscape on the plate	06
County to county, dish to dish	16
Rice and the seasons of the year	30
A thousand and one rice types	34
Citric fruits: oranges, lemons and mandarins	42
Fruits	49
Artichoke from Benicarló	52
Ferraura, *tavella* and *garrofó*	54
Ñora spicy pepper and dried tomatoes	57
Pickles and brines	58
Organic agriculture and gastro-botany	60
The sea and the cuisine of the boats	63
Salted fish, a millenary technique	70
The geography of the *coca* flat breads	74
Mediterranean cheeses	78
Traditional cured meats	82
The truffle of Maestrat and Els Ports	86
Stews, broths and gazpachos	88
Albufera: hunting and fishing	94
Sweet temptations	101
Nougat from Xixona and Alicante	105
Land of ice-cream makers	110
The tiger nut and *horchata* drink	112
Wines and spirits: millenary tradition	116
Other products	124
Recipes	128

Rich, diverse, large, happy land. Crucible of cultures and civilisations through which have passed Punic people, Greeks, Romans, Visigoths and Arabs. A landscape of contrasts whose bright colours have inspired artists and writers. People of an affable and hospitable nature that are characterised by welcoming with open arms visitors who arrive from the most distant points of the planet to enjoy its Mediterranean climate, its beaches, its natural beauty and, of course, its unsurpassable gastronomic richness, a unique and differentiated gastronomy that makes the most of the incredible abundance and diversity of the land.

Fruit, vegetables, fish, seafood, meat and game and farm poultry have been traditionally combined wisely and creatively to achieve a surprisingly varied and tasty cuisine.

The gastronomic journey around the counties of the three provinces of the Valencia Community will provide us with the most unexpected sensations and allow us to discover unique culinary experiences. We will travel in time guided by the ancient civilisations. We will discover ancestral techniques of conserving the food that has come to shape the taste of a people. We will learn how to make dishes that we once thought we were going to lose, a vernacular cuisine that went out of fashion, made a comeback and which today they serve in the finest restaurants.

Coastal cuisine and inland cuisine; rural cuisine and bourgeois cuisine; traditional cuisine and avant-garde cuisine… Distinct aspects of the same gastronomic reality, the authentic treasure of a territory as beautiful as it is varied, the edible materialisation of a landscape that becomes a recipe on the plate.

The landscape on the plate

There was a time in which the recipes that the grannies of yesteryear prepared seemed destined for oblivion. The triumph of the modern, bourgeois cuisine, open to all influences, seemed to relegate those more rural or traditional, everlasting, preparations to the background. For a generation of chefs, especially in the cities, the vernacular cuisine more rooted to the land seemed opposed to modernity.

Fortunately things have changed greatly in the last two decades. The recovery of the gastronomic heritage of the three provinces of the Valencia Community is a fact. With the incentive of improving tourist facilities the serious and decisive commitment was made to improve training in the hotel and catering industry. The contribution of a whole new batch of young chefs, professionally trained in the best schools and centres, has been decisive in the recovery and evaluation of the autochthonous cookbook. Great chefs of modernity and the avant-garde have placed the Valencia Community as a gastronomic benchmark, a worldwide attraction, from the greater respect for traditional cuisine and opening new creative horizons.

For its geographic peculiarities the Valencia Community is a country of great gastronomic contrasts.

A long and characteristically narrow territory, facing the sea, presupposes the primacy of a marine coastal cuisine. The best and most diverse products from fishing are supplied every day in the fish markets thus favouring a particularly rich fish and seafood cuisine.

The Valencia gastronomy is the edible expression of the rich character of its varied geography.

The important fruit and vegetable-growing tradition is a direct inheritance of the Arab age of splendour and the implantation of their irrigation systems. A privileged climate, ideal for the most varied crops, has determined and incomparable richness that translates into a magnificently plural cookbook with hundreds, even thousands, of recipes in which fruit and vegetables are the true protagonists or luxury accompaniments.

Inland the landscape becomes more abrupt. The craggy sierras become natural frontiers between the mountainous systems and the sandy beaches, marshlands and lagoons. Before the tourist, industrial and urban growth of the coastal areas, the interior is much more unpopulated and, in many cases, the economy of its villages is closely linked to the agricultural and livestock sector or the orchard and the countryside.

Different civilisations have left their mark in the local gastronomy. We can find Neolithic vestiges that remind us how they lived in the caves and the first stuttering of agriculture. Iberians, Phoenicians, Greeks and Carthaginians had their settlements here to trade from the maritime ports. The Romans would promote the wines and famous *garum*, this strong sauce made from the juices of

Above, rural pattern.
Below, detail of a beautiful corner of the Valencia lagoon area.

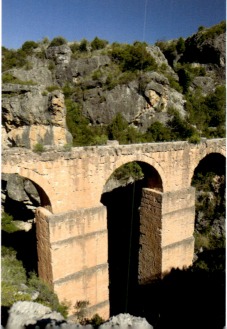

Natural beauties of the inland counties.

blue fish gut in salt all around the Mediterranean. In fact, the taste for salted food has remained as a sign of gastronomic identity. In no other spot in the country is there a culture as deeply-rooted and knowledgeable of this millenary art of conservation of the more or less noble parts of the fish as here.

The cookbook of the Visigoths and Byzantines is not very well known to us. However, the long period of Arab domination left us a rich legacy in both production and preparation of food whose inheritance is still palpable in the orchards and market gardens.

The gastronomy in the counties of the provinces of Castellón, Valencia and Alicante would merit a large encyclopaedia to be able to give each of the different products, recipes or culinary preparations the space they deserve. In each village, in each valley, we come across a different speciality, a special way of preparing the food from the land

The economy of many districts in the mountainous areas of the Valencia Community is based on the agriculture and livestock sector.

that has been preserved over time. An enormous heritage that is a true treasure to discover for the most restless gastronomes.

We could establish geographic routes all over the region following the diverse preparations of the coca flat breads, broths, rice dishes or specialities in cake-making. Not to mention the wines, a sublime expression of the character of the land, a sector that is on the road to recovering the great prestige it enjoyed for centuries, until the phylloxera devastated the vineyards in the mid-19th century.

An alternative route would take the festival calendar as the starting point. Gastronomy is completely linked to traditional celebrations. Patron saint festivals, religious festivals or popular festivals, all of them unavoidably have a dish or recipe to delight the palate.

Lorenzo Millo, the great scholar of Valencia cuisine, stated that to define the gastronomy of this land we should take into account its constant historical and social evolution. Thus, being a more receptive than emigrant community, it has received the most diverse influences that have gradually shaped its complex personality. And, without doubt, will continue doing so, since the

Above, view of the Central Market of Valencia.
Below, fruit shop.

valencian_cuisine

Bucolic landscape on the outskirts of Morella.
Above, artichoke cardoon green leaves. Below, snail seller.

valencian_cuisine

Above, basket of artichokes from Benicarló.
Below, display of paella pans in a local hardware shop.

gastronomy —the products, techniques and recipes— is a living discipline that evolves and which constantly experiences changes in time.

Much more than paella

Nobody doubts it: rice, introduced by the Arabs, has become the most characteristic element of Valencia's gastronomy. Everything appears to indicate that the Muslims did not grow it on a large scale. To eat it, they washed it seven times in hot water and then cooked it in milk or made a type of bread with it that also included millet, broad beans, lentils and green beans.

The paella, this brilliant invention that emerged in the mid-18th century to facilitate the preparation of rice in the countryside for many diners, gave its name to the most international recipe in Spanish cuisine. In the nineteen-seventies it became the unarguable symbol of the developing Spain that welcomed tourism with open arms under the slogan of *"Spain is different"*. Object of conferences, debates and congresses, the paella has come to be the grand totem and taboo of Valencia's gastronomy. A tyrannical supremacy that, sometimes, ends up providing as much pleasure as it does pain. Popularly it is said that here it is easy to lose a friend due to a stupid argument about the inexcusable ingredients of the paella. The critic Antonio Vergara pronounced that "the paella is argued about more than it is eaten".

Its importance is so great that, for many years, the paella, with its sweeping protagonism, has "cannibalised" a gastronomy as rich and varied as that of the Valencia Community. The same Vergara provoked a widespread popular argument when in 1980 he published an article titled "The assassin paella", defending the idea that the oligopoly of the paella marginalised other dishes. With the passing of time, and through solid informative effort, many other traditional rice dishes and recipes have finally had the importance they deserve on the menus of the most well-known restaurants and gaining the favour of the diners.

The paella, totemic icon of Valencian cuisine.

valencian_cuisine

County to county, dish to dish

The enormous richness of products and recipes of the Valencia Community is reflected in the vast culinary heritage of its towns. Here we propose a small outline through the different county cuisines of the provinces of Castellón, Valencia and Alicante.

We begin our tour in the **north of Castellón**, in the beautiful mountainous county of Els Ports. It is an area of typical mountain dishes such as Morellana soup, flan soup, the Christmas meatball, lamb *tombet*, stews and broths, the *recapte* using leftovers, *coca* flat bread *amb xulla* (with cured meat), the Morellana croquettes, hen stuffed with truffles, partridge in pickle or rabbit with snails (*vaquetes*). Among the sweet dishes feature the *rosegons*, macaroons, *arrop i tallaetes*, sweet fig bread and, of course, the *flaons* of Morella cakes.

El Baix Maestrat is, without doubt, one of the most visited counties of Castellón for the attraction of its large tourist centres: Peñíscola, Benicarló, Alcossebre and Vinaròs. All the produce of the sea, especially the prawns from Vinaròs, are protagonists of a succulent and varied marine cuisine, with recipes such as the *suquet* of fish or the *all i pebre* of monkfish. Inland, the cuisine gains in robustness. Typical dishes are the grilled suckling lamb, rice with snails, the stew of Sant Mateu, baked rice, almond soup and the cured meats from the slaughtered pig. Among the sweets: liquor rolls, *pastissets*, fritters, *rosques*, *prims*, sighs and macaroons.

The cuisine is also solid in the towns of **L'Alt Maestrat**. Here feature the broths, the suckling lamb, the *tombet*, grilled meat with *alioli* sauce, rabbit with *rovellon* wild mushroom sauce, the meat of the threshing floor —which was prepared during the threshing season—, the cured meats and hams. In the sweet dishes, junkets, pastry rolls, *cocs amb mel* (with honey), pumpkin cakes, almond cakes, almond flans and *coca celestial*, angel cake.

In **L'Alcalatén** you must try the succulent *tombet* of rabbit and potatoes accompanied by white snails (*vaquetes*), stew *amb pilotes* (with meatballs), chicken and rabbit rice stew, meatball paella, stew of *cardets* (cardoons), cured meats and ham. Desserts: *orelletes*, *codony* flat bread

Mountainous landscape of L'Alt Maestrat, the county in whose culinary and cake-making richness the loyalty to tradition survives.

valencian_cuisine

(quince), *mostillo* with grapes, macaroons, cream cake roll, aniseed pastry rings…

In **La Plana Alta**, paella is the dish par excellence along with black rice, the *arrossejat*, rice stew, baked rice and noodles. All the specialities from the abundant fresh fish that reaches the Puerto del Grao enjoy great popularity. The cocas or flat breads are justifiably renowned, especially the *malfeta* and that of Castellón, which uses potato instead of flour. In the nineteen-eighties a cake-maker from Oropesa created the *oropesinas*, almond cakes that are now very popular. Other sweets are the *rosegons*, *cristines*, *pastissos* of yam, *descàrregues*, almond cakes and *pilotes de frare* (iterally friar's balls).

Among the specialities from **La Plana Baixa** we should especially highlight the marsh rice of Burriana, the *suquet* de peix, the *empedrao*, the mountain paella, the *xulla* or pumpkin stew. For sweets, the rolls of Sant Blai, the Pasqualet, the almond cakes, the coca *malfeta* (iterally badly made), *manjòvenes*, the dessert of San Pascual or the *pilotes de frare*.

The county of **Alt Millars** features the cured meats of the slaughtered pig, porridge, cardoon stew, village stew, wild boar in sauce, lamb fricassee and the dishes with saffron milk caps (here called *rebollones*) from Montanejos. In sweets, the sugared almonds, fig bread, coated fig fritters, Jerusalem artichokes or puff pastries with Chantilly cream and fondant nuts.

In **Viver**, in the Alto Palancia they make saint's rice, with cod and kidney beans. In En Segorbe the famous dishes are the *segorbina* stew, rice *empedrao* and the cured meats, as

A moment of rest during the cherry harvest close to La Salzadella.

well as specialities with cod, such as the *ajoaceite de palo* sauce. Other county specialities are trout with almond, "poor man's" potatoes, rice with cabbage and ribs and traditional cured meats. Here, of course, they cook with oil from the Espadán range, which is obtained from the local serran variety of olives. Among the sweets: *cocotes*, almond pastries, sighs, *orelletes*, iced cakes, *cristina* cakes and *torrijas* (fried bread with milk and honey).

The beauty of the bright almond trees in flower enlivens the fields during the winter foreboding the arrival of spring.

Now in the province of Valencia, in **Camp de Morvedre**, the different rice preparations stand out: paella, *arròs negre* (black rice), stew of *fesols i naps* (with kidney beans and turnips), *empedrat*, chick pea broth and meat stew. Top-quality cured meats are produced and the cherries of Serra are famous. Among the sweets feature the *orelletes* with honey or the coca *en llanda*. The sugared almonds and nougats from Casinos are made in the traditional.

valencian_cuisine

The cuisine of the Valencia area reflects a deep love of all things rural and for the best ingredients of the market garden

valencian_cuisine

In **Camp de Túria** the different types of rice are traditional dishes: paellas of chicken and rabbit, of cabbage and ribs, the *arròs amb fesols i naps* (rice with kidney beans and turnips) and *arròs amb bledes* (Swiss chard). Also typical is the *caragolà* (snails in spicy sauce), the yam cakes, the *congrets*, the *panquemados* buns and the *orelletes*.

La Serrania del Turia (The Hills) is one of the most mountainous and irregular counties in the entire Community. Its cuisine is solid and features the *churra* stew, cardoon stew, porridge, breadcrumbs and bacon, and the mountain gazpacho.

In the corner of **Ademuz**, an authentic "exclave" of the Valencia Community, we find typical dishes of mountain cuisine: maize porridge, broth, vetches or rice with cod and broad beans, broth and the village stew. Of merited fame are its autochthonous varieties of tomatoes and apples.

In **L'Horta**, as well as the traditional paellas, you must try the paella of *fetge de bou* (with chick peas, endives and bull's liver), the vegetable paella, rice with cod and the *rossejat* con morcilla sausage, *blanquets*, *garreta*, pig's trotters and meatballs.

The most famous festival of the county of **La Hoya de Buñol-Chiva** is the *Tomatina*, which is held on the last Wednesday of August and becomes an authentic battle in which tomatoes are used as ammunition. Among the most outstanding dishes of this county are the *tajà* cakes, the cod with *mojete* sauce, the herb stew, cardoon stew, breadcrumbs and bacon, the traditional *gachamiga* flour tortilla and the *rin ran* with cod.

In **Utiel-Requena** you must try the gazpachos, porridge, *gachamiga*, *ajoarriero*, *morteruelo* stew, broth and stew. The *alajú* is a very peculiar sweet of Arab origin, very popular in Cuenca, made with almonds and honey.

Rice dishes are the epicentre of the gastronomy of **La Ribera Baixa**. Sueca is the main rice producer in Spain. As well as the paella, baked rice, rice stew, black rice or with seafood, famous

Valencia wines are a perfect reflection of the land where they come from and the character of its people.

Panorama of the district of Tuéjar,
in the mountainous county of Los Serranos,
an area of gazpachos, stews and morteruelo stews

are the *all i pebre* of eels and the *espardenyà*, similar to *all i pebre* but with the addition of chicken, duck or rabbit. For sweets, the *coques fines* and of pumpkin, Christmas cakes, and rolls of Sant Blai and Arnadí.

In **La Ribera Alta** you must try the cuisine of the marshland, with all its varieties of rice, the *all i pebre* of eels and the *espardenyà*. In sweets, the pastissets of yam, the panquemaos of Alberic and the fogasses.

Popular in **Canal de Navarrés** are the gazpacho, the cod with *mojete* sauce or *bullio* and the aromatised rice dishes with mountain herbs. In cake-making, the yam pie, *torticas*, *bizcochás*, *hogasas*, aniseed rolls and the Easter chocolate figures.

The valley of **Ayora-Cofrentes** features mountain gazpachos, stews, broths, *morteruelo* stew and *calducho* stew, as well as the *ajetao*, *ajotonto*, *trigo picao* with wheat and

the *gachamigas* made with breadcrumbs. In sweets, the *grullos*, *aguamiel* and macaroons. The honey from Jalance is an absolute must to try.

In **La Safor** it is obligatory to try the noodles from Gandía and the extensive assortment of rice dishes. Also typical are the *figatells*, the stuffed flat breads, the flat breads a la *calfó*, the *pebreres farcides*, prawn with Swiss chard, flat breads de *dacsa* and the *pastissos*.

The rice dishes (baked, stew, paella…), the *pericana* sauce and baked flat bread, with cured meats and mushrooms form part of the popular cookbook of **La Vall d'Albaida**. For dessert, *pastissets* of yam and egg yolk fondant.

The baked casserole is the most typical dish of **La Costera**. Also popular are the paella, the *arròs amb fesols* i naps (with kidney beans and turnips), rice stew with Swiss chard and chick peas, stew, the Valencia stew at Easter and the *gachamiga* made with breadcrumbs of La Font de Figuera. In sweets, the *arnadí* with pumpkin, the *almoixàvena*, the *bones taronges* (good oranges) from Xàtiva (with unsalted cheese, eggs and flour), the *marqués*, cake, *nevasa*, the flat bread *en llanda*, the tartlets of yam and the *sequillos*. Excellent olive oil of the manzanilla, alfafara or blanqueta varieties.

In the province of **Alicante** we start our gastronomic route in La Marina Alta. Among its typical dishes we can find diverse and original rice recipes (rice with barley and fish, rice with cod, baked, with cardoons…), *borreta* of tuna, *mullador de pelleta*, octopus stew, *llanda* from Calpe, *llandeta* from Dénia, seafood casserole, *figatells*, *bull* sausage stew… Among the desserts, varied sweet flat breads, tarts, cakes, *arrop i tallaetes*, yam cakes…

Marina Baixa is one of the favourite destinations of the Costa Blanca. Among its most typical dishes feature the wheat stew, maize ball stew, fish stew, the *suquets*, *llandetas*, the *borreta*, the

The oranges of La Safor are deservedly famous.
On the right, market day in Oliva.

pebrereta talladeta, *espencat, bullit*, the *cru* of cod, the stuffed *coques farcides* (flat breads) and the *minxos* pancakes. Among the desserts, the *coca boba*, rolls of Sant Blai from Tàrbena, the pastries of Sant Blai from Benidorm, the flat bread cake, *borreguets*, *sequillos* or biscuits from Benimantell.

In the northeast of the province, the *Comptat* or **County of Cocentaina** offers us succulent, mountain dishes, such as stew, rabbit with garlic, broths, diverse flat breads, *fassedures de dacsa* (maize balls), the *pericana*, *borreta* and chopped wheat. For desserts: *crelletes*, fried figs, rolls, *carcanyols* and *sequillos*. Very popular liqueurs are made here such as Herbero or the Coffee liqueur which, in summer has crushed ice lemon with caramel added and becomes "La mentira", the lie.

L'Alcoià is an inland and mountainous county. Traditional dishes: musician's stew, notary's stew, flat breads of flour and tomato, *borreta* (spinach and cod), *pericana*, *espardenyes* (sardines in breadcrumbs), fresh anchovy croquettes (*aladroc*), *sabater* rice (shoemaker, with vegetables), *figatells*, *mullador* of rabbit… The sugared almonds are typical of Alcoy. Other typical sweets of the county are sugar-coated nuts, nougats, *pastelitos de Gloria* with yam, sweet toasted pine nuts and liquor rolls.

L'Alacantí is the county that includes the districts around the capital and the small island of Tabarca. Of its varied gastronomy we highlight the *espencat, borretas* of cod, sardine and onion flat breads, salted foods, *campellera* noodles, *giraboix* stew, *torruana* stew, gazpacho with *ñora* pepper and diverse rice dishes. Among the desserts, the nougats and ice creams of Xixona, the almond cupcakes, the *pà beneït* (blessed bread) of Torremanzanas and the unfilled fritters.

L'Alt Vinalopó. Typical dishes: stew, *gachamigas* with breadcrumbs, salted gazpacho, Manchego gazpacho, rice with rabbit and snails, stews, *olleta del camp* (country stew), stuffed meatballs, *borreta* of cod, rice stew… Desserts: *coquetes*, almond cakes, *mantecaos* (almonds and lard), sweet rolls, *tortà* and yam cakes.

El Vinalopó Mitjà. Typical dishes: *borreta*, *torta* gazpachos, *fassedures*, heaven's soup (potatoes, cod, eggs and tomato), *giraboix* stew, *moje noveldero* (anchovy stew), *tortas monfortinas* of sardine, *bollitori* of cod… Desserts: *sequillos*, *toñas*, cupcakes, *perusas*, *coca boba*, love rolls, tarts, almond and lard sweets, *rajadillos*, *suspiros*, *monjávenas* and liquor rolls.

The most outstanding feature of Valencia cuisine is its enormous richness, a loyal reflection of its varied landscape.

El Baix Vinalopó. Typical dishes: rice with crust, rice and tripe, *putxero amb tarongetes* (cooked with meatballs), gazpacho of grouper, *blanquillo* of monkfish, fish soup, *gacha-miga*, *pipes i carasses* (cod with *ñora* peppers), grey mullet from the Laguna del Hondo, flat breads, *pà torrat* (toasted bread typical at Easter). Desserts: *tortà* from Elche, *pamfígol*, dates, *Dulces de Crevillent*.

El Baix Segura is the southernmost county of Alicante, neighbouring Murcia. Among its typical dishes we find artichoke salad, rice with crust, rice of the three "puñaos" or fists, rice of the donkey, "bacalao meneao" - "drunk" rice, soup of *agramaor*, porridge with syrup, wheat *gachamigas* with breadcrumbs and potatoes, tripe broth, "drunk" black guan stew, *hormigones*. And in the sweets, *almojábenas* (with cheese), *torta boba*, pumpkin cake with honey, macaroons, *mantecás* of almond and lard, *tortas escaldadas* with pastry and *pasteles de Gloria* cakes.

The Mediterranean character impregnates the gastronomy of the Community. Beautiful views of the picturesque island of Tabarca.

Rice and the seasons of the year

Rice was first cultivated in southeast Asia, India and China approximately 15,000 years ago. In the Mediterranean zone it was introduced by the Greeks, although on the Iberian peninsula it was the Arabs who consolidated it as a crop; according to old documents from the 8th century rice was already being produced in Sueca. In the first known medieval cookbooks, *"El llibre del Sent Soví"* or *"El Llibre del Coch"*, appear the first rice recipes, mainly used as a dessert or originally cooked in almond milk.

Rice (*Oryza sativa*) is a grass plant whose cultivation is restricted to temperate climates and swampy and floodable lands, such as the deltas of rivers, mud flats or marshy coastland. In the Valencia Community the cultivation of rice is widely extended along the peripheral zones of the lagoons. In the districts of Sueca, Sollana, Cullera and Silla is grown approximately three-quarters of all the rice produced in the Community.

In 1997 the process was started to establish an "Arroz de Valencia" Designation of origin, the regulation of which was passed in 2000, to endorse the origin and quality of the rice grown in the protected areas. The brands covered by the Designation of Origin can be recognised in the shop by the label on the back with the logo and code number that identifies them.

The "Arroz de Valencia" Designation of Origin only protects rice catalogued as Extra and belonging to three varieties: bahía, sénia and bomba, three types of rice perfectly acclimatised to the conditions of the Valencia lagoon. The three varieties are of Japanese origin and are perfect for ensuring the grain absorbs to the

The colour of the rice fields varies chromatically following the rhythm of the seasons.

valencian_cuisine

maximum the flavours of the stock in which they are cooked.

The tasks relating to the annual cycle of growing rice transform the landscape of the lagoon according to a calendar of agricultural practices. In January the rice fields are flooded in order to desalt the land and, at the end of this month, the tractors begin the mulching (*fanguejat*), an operation that consists of mixing and preparing the soil, flooded with a low level of water, with the help of the rear cage of the tractors.

Around April the fields begin to dry and work begins on smoothing and ploughing the land.

After these operations, the fields are gradually flooded again. In May the rice is sown. Currently, the system of replanting the *guaixcs* or previously cultivated stems in *planters* is very rare, given that it is a manual and costly job. The most commonly used sowing method consists of scattering the seeds with the help of a device in the form of a funnel attached to the tractor.

Around June the first shoots begin to appear and the waters of the rice fields take on a greenish hue. During July the rice grows notably and the farmers drop the flooding levels of the fields in order to remove the weeds. This operation is known as *eixugó*. The marshland acquires a golden colour during August, as the ears of rice ripen.

During September and October the fields gradually dry and the harvest begins. In the past, the harvesting was done by hand using a sickle. The ears were grouped together forming *garbas* and, after the trimming, the grain was separated from the straw by means of a thresher on a threshing floor. Today, the modern crop machines do the harvesting and thresh the ears at the same time. Later, they transport the rice to the cooperative farm installations.

Above, detail of the ripening of the ears of rice.
On the right, view of the flooded rice fields.

The rice is dried in industrial dryers so that it loses the moisture it contains. The treatment is completed with the husking —separation of the husk from the grain— and whitening processes, the latter consisting of scraping the grains in a mill with a porous stone that smooths the surface, thus obtaining a whiter grain and with greater capacity for absorption. The last stage consists of selecting the grains, separating the split or small ones, to establish the different qualities.

After the harvest, the straw is burnt before the autumn rainfall begins. As the saying goes, *"rice is planted in water, is grown in water and is cooked in water"*. During November and December the fields are flooded again and the cycle begins anew.

valencian_cuisine

A thousand and one rice types

The Valencia rice cookbook is unique in the world. Hundreds —and even thousands— of preparations —with different ingredients and techniques of preparation— make up a singular autochthonous gastronomy in which the vegetables from the market garden and the most diverse ingredients from the sea, mountain or farmyard become the true stars.

The recipients used in preparing the rice determine the final result of the dish. Thus, the flat earthenware casseroles dishes are ideal for baked rice, a very old speciality that was prepared traditionally in a baker's oven in order to have the meal ready for the workers in the countryside, conserving the heat until the moment they finished work. On adding just the right amount of stock, the rice remains hot without the cooking point being over affected. The same does not occur in the preparation of rice stews. In this case, the earthenware recipients —used

valencian_cuisine

traditionally— require the rice to consume it immediately, since the heat it holds ends up causing the overcooking of the grain.

Iron pots, high and round, are perfect for cooking rice stews. They were used on the boats to prepare the sailors' meal, their high walls avoiding the swaying of the waves from spilling the liquid from cooking the fish in which later the rice was cooked. The typical iron pots continue to be irreplaceable for preparing stews, *olletes,* and soupy rice dishes in many places.

The paella always deserves a new paragraph when speaking of the rice of Valencia and for this reason we have dedicated the following pages.

On the left and above, the hundred-year-old rice restaurant La Pepica, on the beach of La Malvarosa. On the right, rice varieties.

valencian_cuisine

The paella step by step

1, 2 & 3

Prepare a wood fire and leave the charcoal burning, so that when adding small branches the intensity of the flames varies according to the taste of the paella maker. The paella pan is specially designed to ensure that the heat of the fire spreads as quickly as possible, thus resulting in quick evaporation of the stock and a uniform cooking, more so if the layer of rice is particularly thin. This is why they use large size paella dishes when preparing them for many diners. When it is not possible to cook them over a wood fire a diffuser must be used to ensure a uniform cooking. Heat the oil with the garlic to aromatise it and sauté all the meats until they brown.

4 Once browned, remove the meats to the edges of the paella dish. In the centre, sauté the chopped green beans and the peeled and chopped tomatoes.

5 Add the threads of saffron and the green beans. Season, if you want, with a little paprika, salt and pepper, and stir well.

6 Add the necessary water (calculate double the amount of water to rice) and measure with a stick or wooden spoon. The humidity mark on the stick will show the level of stock required. Later, add more water and raise the intensity of the flames adding small branches to the fire.

7 Leave the stock to reduce on a medium-high flame for around 30 minutes, until obtaining the amount of reduced stock that the humidity mark shows on the stick or wooden spoon. This way of measuring the exact amount stock is very practical. Nevertheless, expert paella chefs do not need it: they know how to calculate the stock necessary simply by being guided visually by the marks of the rivets on the handles of the paella dish. **8 & 9** Add the rice and cook it on a medium flame for the first 10 minutes. Later, lower the intensity of the flame and cook it for another eight minutes. **10** Remove the paella from the fire and leave it to rest for a few minutes before serving. If you want, you can eat it without plates, with each diner eating the rice directly from the paella with a spoon.

valencian_cuisine

Citric fruits:
oranges, lemons and mandarins

Although today its economic importance is very minor, in reality the first citric fruit to reach European lands was the citron. Originally from southeast Asia, the citron (*Citrus medica*) reached Europe via the journeys of Alexander the Great. In Rome it was already grown around the 3rd century AD and the first crops in this country could

be dated at the beginning of the 7th century. The citron flowered several times a year and always had flowers and fruits on the tree.

In 714 the Muslims arrived in the province of Castellón. A new period began for the farming of the area, marked by the redistribution of the large estates, the establishment of new species, such as the bitter orange (*Citrus aurantium*) or the grapefruit or *pummelo*, and the improvement in farming techniques: reproduction by seed in nurseries, pruning, fertilising, clearing… The Muslims also developed innovative and efficient irrigation systems by means of constructing canals, drains, waterwheels and reservoirs. The citron and the lime (*Citrus aurantifolia*) were two most used citric fruits in the refined Andalusian cuisine. The bitter orange tree had an ornamental function. However, the delicate perfume of the orange blossom was obligatorily present in the most beautiful gardens and mosques. The orange blossom water was used to make perfumes and aromatise sweets and refreshing drinks. The lemon tree (*Citrus limon*) would reach the Iberian peninsula around the second half of the 11th century.

One of the oldest bibliographical references to the cultivation of citric fruits in the Valencia Com-

On the left, detail of the juiciness of Valencia oranges.
On the right, mandarins about to be picked

valencian_cuisine

munity is the quote that appears in the "*Regiment de la Cosa Pública*" by Francesc Eiximenis (1340-1409) in which the Franciscan extols the beauty of the orange and lemon orchards of the Levantine regions.

However surprising it may seem to us, the growing of the sweet orange (*Citrus sinensis*), originating from the regions of southeast China, had no commercial importance in the Mediterranean zone until the 16th century. The Portuguese Vasco de Gama introduced the new varieties of sweet oranges into Europe two years after his voyage to China in 1518. From then on, as recognition of its exotic origin, they were known by the popular name of *Chinese oranges*.

Above, different tasks in mandarin picking.
On the left, detail of a lemon tree.

Picking the citric fruits.

The acclimatisation of the sweet orange in the hot Mediterranean lands was spectacular: as from the end of the 18th century the first commercial plantations were established in eastern Spain, where it would soon become the most charismatic fruit of its gastronomic landscape. Just as father Antoni Josep Cavanilles recounts in his "*Observaciones sobre la historia, geografía, agricultura, población y frutos del Reyno de Valencia*" (1797), the first commercial sweet orange plantations were introduced in 1781 in Bassa del Rei, part of Carcaixent and was the result of an initiative by a priest, father Vicente Monzó along with two friends, the chemist Jacinto Bodí and the scribe Carlos Maseres. A few decades later cultivation began on the Plana de Castellón.

The gradual development of the cultivations as from 1880 was due to a large extent to the

new agricultural investments by the Valencia bourgeoisie, the application of a steam engine to raise the underground water and the improvement in communications, basically ports and railways, which enormously aided the trade of the citric fruits. Orange-growing extended all along the coastal strip of the gulf of Valencia, from the Plana de Castellón to Safor, mainly on dry land that took as its limits the historic irrigated land or the marshlands and the highest foothills to the west. The old dry lands ended up transformed into irrigated land due to the excavation of wells and the installation of waterwheels and steam engines.

The successive crises of other crops such as cereals, mulberries or, above all, grapes, resulted in the expansion of the orange groves in the region. Exports to European countries increased greatly until halted by the outbreak of the First World War. At the end of the conflict, the sector

The tradition of growing citric fruits in the Valencia Community enjoys recognition and prestige the world over.

experienced another age of splendour thanks to improvements in transport. After the Spanish Civil War and the Second World War difficult years were once again experienced. The sector was able to revive itself in production figures during the 1950s and 60s. 1968 will be remembered for the plague of a disease called "sadness", which affected more than one million fruit trees. In the 1970s many orange trees were replaced by distinct varieties of mandarins (mandarins, satsumas and clementines).

Entry into the European Union gave a boost to the stability of exports. In 1999 the Regulatory Council of the "Cítricos Valencianos" Protected Geographic Indication was created to protect, promote and guarantee the excellence of the fruit.

The big problem in the sector these days is the enormous imbalance between the price of origin of the fruit and the market price that the consumer ends up paying. The changing consumer habits, ecological and sustainable production methods and new technologies, which offer the possibility of buying recently picked oranges directly from the farmer by internet, are some of the new challenges that the sector must face in a complex and competitive market in which, despite everything, citric fruits continue leading world fruit production.

Citric fruits from Valencia have a Protected Geographic Indication.

Fruits

1 Pomegranates

Originating from the Middle East, pomegranate-growing (*Punica granatum*) gradually spread and became acclimatised around the Mediterranean basin more than one thousand years ago. In the south of Alicante, Campo de Elche, Crevillente and Albateraalcanza, the molar variety is most common, which enjoys international prestige for its characteristic sweetness and absence of pips. More than 2,100 hectares are cultivated here with an approximate annual consumption of 40,000 tons, which is harvested from September to December.

2 Avocados

Although the first avocados reached the Botanical Gardens of Valencia more than four centuries ago, avocado cultivation is relatively modern and dates back to the late 1970s. Today the production areas are spread between Callosa d'en Sarrià, Altea, Polop, Gandía, Benifaió, Alginet, Picassent, Faura and other small towns. It is a fruit that lasts a long time on the tree, where it can be for up to four months. Ripening does not start until the fruit has been picked. Harvesting takes place from March to July.

3 Kaki from La Ribera del Xúquer

The Designation of Origin Kaki de la Ribera del Xúquer protects the quality of the *bright* red variety of kakis, whether with soft pulp (*classic*) or hard pulp (*persimmon*). Its cultivation originates in the almost anecdotal plantation of some seeds in the town of El Carlet. Later, in the early 1970s, the first plantation was grafted in the district of L'Alcudia. Today the annual production figures have reached 25,000 tons.

4 Cherry tree landscape

The blossoming of the cherry trees at the end of the winter transforms the colour of the fields and gives them a magical and magnificent character. Towns in Castellón such as

valencian_cuisine

Caudiel, in the county of Alto Palancia and La Salzadella, in Baix Maestrat, have made cherries a sign of identity of their gastronomy. Also highly appreciated are the mountain cherries from Alicante, which possess a Specific Designation. The harvesting begins in late May and early June.

5 Medlar from Callosa

From November to December, the medlars begin to flower covering the fruit trees with bunches of white flowers and impregnating the fields with their delicate aroma. Harvesting begins in early spring, although it can be delayed until mid-June.

The medlars from Callosa d'en Sarrià have a Designation of Origin that protects their quality and represents more than half of the total national production. There are numerous varieties, both historic and new, the main ones being *algar* or *agerie* and *nadal*.

6 Wrapped grapes from Vinalopó

In the 1920s, a farmer from the Valle del Vinalopó wrapped the bunches of grapes growing on his stocks with a paper bag in an attempt to protect them from a plague. By coincidence, he realised that the bag not only protected the grape from the insects and avoided the direct fumigation of insecticides but also protected them from the inclemency of the weather and delayed their ripening. The *Uva de Mesa Embolsada de Vinalopó* has a Designation of Origin that guarantees that, for at least sixty days, the bunches are protected by a pure shiny cellulose paper bag. The varieties protected by the D.O. are *ideal*, with light flavour of muscatel and *aledo*. This latter variety, later in harvesting, can be wrapped for 4 months and the grape is eaten to celebrate the chiming of the clock on New Year's Eve.

7 Dates from Elche

The introduction of the palm trees, originally from the Middle East, dates back to the Phoenician period and experienced their greatest age of splendour during Arab domination. With more than 200,000 examples, the palm plantation of Elche is the largest in Europe. Also important is the palm plantation of Orihuela, immortalised by the poetry of Miguel Hernández. Attached only by an esparto grass belt, raised some twenty metres up the trunk of the palm tree and skilfully handling their machetes, the palm tree workers pick the bunches of dates while singing traditional songs (*cançons del munyir*). Once picked, the dates are left to dry in the sun over some esparto matting. Harvesting is done from October to December.

valencian_cuisine

Artichoke of Benicarló

The production area of the artichoke of Benicarló extends along the coastal flatlands of the county of Baix Maestrat, in the province of Castellón. Specifically, its cultivation area is spread between the towns of Benicarló, Càlig, Peñíscola and Vinaròs.

The influence of the Mediterranean has a beneficial effect on these lands, saving them from strong oscillations in temperature and enabling the artichoke to grow consistently, round and compact. These special microclimatic characteristics also ensure that the artichokes from the area possess an extraordinary resistance and that they last longer than normal without undermining their quality, delaying the blackening produced by the oxidising ferments contained in the vegetable itself.

The "Alcachofa de Benicarló" Designation of origin and its specific regulation were passed on the 18th of September 1998. In November 2003 it was declared Protected Designation of Origin by the European Union.

To recognise it in the market we must check on its characteristic flattened and compact shape and its peculiar dimple. It should also be identified with the anagram of the *Consejo Regulador*, the regulating council.

On the left and above, details of artichokes of Benicarló.
On the right, harvesting in the field.

valencian_cuisine

Ferraura, tavella and garrofó

One of the most frequent complaints you hear when someone wants to prepare an authentic paella outside of the Valencia Community is the enormous difficulty they have in finding *ferraura*, *tavella* and *garrofó* in the markets. These three ingredients may be totally unknown for the less initiated and that is why they merit a brief introduction.

In Valencia cuisine the use of flat green beans (*bajoques* or *bajoquetes*) and all types of kidney beans (*fesols*) is very generalised.

Green or as a pulse they are protagonists of an extensive traditional cookbook that includes dishes as emblematic as stews, broths and *fesoladas* (bean stews), *bullit*, *arròs amb fesols i naps* (rice with kidney beans and turnips) and, of course, paella.

The officially accepted recipe for Valencia paella includes, as we have said, *ferraura, tavella* and *garrofó*. The *ferraura*, also called *bajocó* in some counties, is a type of green bean shaped like a horseshoe. The *tavella* is shelled in the form of small green beans with a kidney shape and are very aromatic. The *garrofó* is given names as distinctive as the "sugared almond bean" or the "Lima bean". It is a bean plant similar to that of the broad bean and is generally used when tender.

Other types of beans that are usually included in the paella, according to season, are the *rochet* (*roiget* or *rotjet*), which gets its name from its characteristic reddish aspect, and the *manteca* or *mantequeta*, a very tender and buttery type of bean —m*anteca* in Spanish— which is easily identified by the attractive creamy yellow colour its pods.

1. Roget or Rochet. **2.** Garrofó. **3.** Ferraura.
4. Manteca. **5.** Perona. **6.** Tavella.

Ñora peppers and dried tomatoes

Ñoras are dried peppers of the *"capsicuum anuum"* variety, of a blunt and rounded shape. They are distinguished from other peppers both for their characteristic shape and for the peculiar flavour they acquire after drying. The most appreciated in the whole Community are those produced in the county of Vega Baja and, very particularly, those that are dried in Guardamar del Segura.

After picking, the ñoras of Guardamar are placed over the fine sand of the outlet of the Segura and are covered. The sand maintains and spreads the heat at night during the month that the process lasts. The natural drying, without using ovens, differentiates these ñoras or "ball peppers" from the rest of the national production.

Ñoras are major secondary players in the traditional Valencia cookbook in many rice dishes, stews, sauce bases and sauces, the *salmorreta* sauce being the most well-known of these.

Tomatoes dried under the scorching summer sun acquire a strong, robust and distinctive flavour. After ten or twelve days of drying, they are conserved in salt or oil. They reach a very high price in the markets. The traditional *esmorçaet*, the breakfast that charged up the batteries of the farmworkers of Alicante in mid-morning, consisted of a revitalising combination of fried dried tomatoes with a fried egg and a sardine *de casco*, with tomato and garlic

On the left, ñoras and dried tomatoes. Above, strings of ñoras in the market. Below, dried tomatoes in olive oil.

valencian_cuisine

Pickles and brines

The use of brines (salmorres) dates back to the remotest antiquity and is closely linked to the salt trade in the millenary salt works of the Levantine coast. Brine is an ancestral method of food conservation by means of a very simple preparation based on water and salt that was already known by the Phoenicians, Greeks and Romans.

The preparation of pickles is very similar to that of brines. The basic difference is that they use vinegar as the conserving product.

Brines and pickles are very popular in the three provinces to conserve all types of garden produce and have historically formed part of the traditional mid-morning breakfast of farmworkers.

Different types of olives with different dressings and assorted pickles: an ingredient that cannot be missing from a well-laid table.

Olives, capers, onions, cucumbers, peppers, tomatoes, cauliflower, beetroot, carrot… The most diverse market produce of the orchard features in a colourful catalogue of brines and pickles that are usually eaten as appetizers before meals.

Among the most original we should mention those made with caper stems or the *raïm de pastor* (pastor's grape), based on cat's claw, a very common plant on paths and rocky spots that was traditionally used to combat acidity in the stomach. Also surprising for their originality are the tender nuts in brine, which are prepared in some towns in Marina Baixa and the County of Cocentaina.

valencian_cuisine

Organic and gastro-botanical agriculture

The spectacular increase in the demand for organically produced products has met with a response in a sector of Valencia farmers aware of the need to respect the environment and health of the consumer. Organic agriculture is based on respect for the cycle of products and avoids the use of fertilisers, pesticides and other chemical products.

Gastro-botany is a new discipline that studies and commercialises vegetable varieties that are outside the traditional circuits. The pioneering company in this field is located in Elche and bases its business on the commercialisation of fresh dates. Due to their geographic location and late harvest, the dates of Elche are the only fresh dates in the world at the moment they are picked. They also work with unknown citric fruits (limequat, calamondin, Buddha's hand, dragonfly, finger lime…) and fruit and vegetables from the desert, such as land algae, glacier lettuce, carissas or Natal plum, and desert strawberries, small red fruits with the aroma of jasmine… A whole world of new ideas in vegetables to discover.

A rising tendency: the love of more natural products avoiding the use of pesticides and chemical substances.

The sea and the cuisine of the boats

Historically, not only the coastal villages have shown their devotion to the sea and its products in the rich traditional seafaring gastronomy of the Community. The passion for the typical cuisine of the fishermen has also always been present in the towns further away from the coast thanks to the figure of the muleteers, who transported fresh fish and seafood on the backs of their mules and horses over steep routes inland, on some occasions using the ice from the occasional winter and spring snowfalls which was kept in original stone structures called *pous de neu* (snow wells) or *caves* (caves). It is not unusual, therefore, that some seafaring specialities are still today authentic signs of identity of the gastronomy of towns well away from the sea.

Dedication to the arts of navigation and fishing date back to the period of the Iberians and trade with Rome. The popularity of the *garum*

The best fresh fish and seafood can be enjoyed throughout the coastal region of the Valencia Community.

valencian_cuisine

sauce, made with fermented blue fish, also enabled the ceramic industries to flourish to make amphorae and recipients to transport it along with wines and oils. Additionally, the prestige that tuna-based products enjoyed in the metropolis favoured the development of tunny fishing along these coastlines.

Later, the fishermen's guilds spread in the distinct coastal ports. Skill in sailing made the presence of fishermen from Valencia a regular occurrence in distant fishing grounds, such as the Balearics, Canaries or African coasts. In the 1920s, with the popularisation of motor boats, the art of *bou* and dragnet fishing was consolidated and many fishermen's colonies were established in many other places on the national coastline, originating from Valencia, Alicante or Castellón. In the 1950s the fishing fleet of Santa Pola, with more than 200 boats, was considered the largest in the Spanish Mediterranean.

Arrival of the boats in the fish market loaded with a large variety of fish that characterise Valencia marine cuisine.

This historic tradition has resulted in an exquisite marine cuisine which is based on the full use of the sea's resources, from the humblest of small fish, ideal for marine stews, stocks and soups, to the most sought-after delicacies. All the cooking techniques of fish are present in the traditional marine cookbook of the Community: roasted, boiled, stewed, fried, pickled… A very popular and common cooking method should be highlighted, however. It is a *sofrito,* a sauce base

valencian_cuisine

On the left, beautiful panorama of the rocky coast of the island of Tabarca. Above, Santa Pola. Below, gull.

valencian_cuisine

of onion, garlic and tomato, to which is added the fish, covered with a small amount of stock or water and left to boil briefly. With this same technique, although with distinct ingredients, we find many similar specialities with diverse names: *sucs, suquets, cassoles, cruets, nugats*… We should also mention the *llandes* or *llandetes*, recipes in which the fish is baked in a metallic dish from which it gets this name.

It would be impossible to sum up here the immense repertoire that makes up the gastronomic heritage of the Community's marine cuisine. Naturally, rice dishes in all their forms of preparation have become the emblem of Valencia marine cuisine. Noodles also enjoy great standing, whether they are *rossejats*, slightly browned before cooking them, or *a banda*, like rice, or as a stew. Special mention should be made of the *fideuà*, which in Gandía has its unarguable world capital.

Other marine recipes replace the eel with grey mullet (*llissa*), monkfish or sea bass in the traditional *allipebre*, combine cardoons with calamari or octopus or propose lavish baroque dishes such as the octopus stew (*putxero de polp*). The mere number of the most popular marine specialities would be interminable.

Many of these recipes recover the tradition of the cuisine the fishermen themselves produced on board, a basic style of cooking that was later popularised in the guest houses and taverns of the ports. Over the *burguera* or stove, and in the embers of the charcoal, they roasted *cabets*, *gerrets*, sardines, fresh anchovies, mackerels and *jurioles*. They also cooked red mullet, before it became one of the most sough-after delicacies in the market, or the *eixumorat* fish or octopus, dried outdoors for 10 or 12 hours.

In the iron cauldron first were sautéed some cloves of garlic and a ñora pepper, which was later put to one side for the sauce base, and the fish

was placed in layers: first those with the most consistent meat (greater weever, Atlantic stargazer, conger eel, *rascassa*, skate…) and later the softer ones (mackerels, *martinetes*, *rafets*…). Potatoes, crabs and shrimps were added. The fish was cooked for about 20 minutes and seasoned with a dressing of vinegar, garlic and oil and stock. The soup was then served, previously thickened with a good sauce base. In the traditional cuisine of La Marina it was called *sopa de piló* if it was thick with a lot of fried bread or *sopa de galgo* if it was lighter. Rice *a banda* (slightly browned before cooking) or *fideuà* was also prepared in a large pot —paella pans were never used on the boat because, on being flat, the stock would easily spill with the swaying of the waves— and they were always served soupy.

The love of seafood of the people of Valencia is rewarded by the extensive and delicious offer that the great marine larder affords. Among many others, we must mention here the giant prawns from Vinaròs and Guardamar, the striped prawns from Dènia, the lobsters, sea urchins, clams *espardenyes*, *caixetes* or date mussels.

Fish and seafood feature in hundreds of traditional recipes of the marine cuisine of the coastline of Castellón, Valencia and Alicante.

valencian_cuisine

Salted fish, a millenary technique

Borreta, *bull* stew, *pebreretes*, *pericana*, *espencat*, hotpot of *sangatxo*… They are traditional dishes of Alicante cuisine, the province that can feel proud of boasting the title of the number one consumer of salted food, not only in Spain but in all Europe. Nevertheless, the disappearance of tunny fisheries on this coastline (the last one was on the island of Tabarca, in 1960) and the gradual increase in the price of quality salted food has meant that consumer figures have gradually dropped over the last few decades. Despite this, salted food continues to be an unarguable sign of identity of the traditional gastronomy of the Alicante counties.

The elaboration of salted food has a millenary tradition. Its production experienced an age of splendour during the Roman period and was closely linked to the elaboration and trade of the mythical *garum*. Different archaeological sites show that the production process of salted food of 2,500 years ago did not differ much from today.

Each type of fish and each part of the animal requires a technique and special care to achieve the desired flavour and texture. The same occurs in reverse, in the process of desalting. Each chef must learn to find the exact amount of salt desired for each piece.

A real expert must know how to differentiate between traditionally-made quality salted food and a false piece, made with frozen tuna from the Gulf of Mexico processed in drying tunnels.

Another subject that must be passed to become a good gourmet of salted food consists of learning to recognise the sixteen different types of tuna salting, from the humble *sangatxo* to the select *mormo* (a type of fillet situated on the head

Salted food in the stand of the Central Market of Valencia, one of the best places In the world to buy this product.

of the fish) or the fleshy part of the neck, (oilier) as well as the heart, the *budellet* (tripe), the *espineta* or the *faseres* (the gelatinous membranes that surround the tuna's eyes). Everything is eaten.

The popular *mojama* comes from the parts called *descargados* and *descargamentos*, beneath the back of the tuna. It is the driest part of the fish and is easy to cut and has dark, shiny colour. When frozen light tuna is used (*yellowfin*), the colour is fainter and the flavour less intense.

The prestigious *tonyina de sorra*, also known as *ijada*, *ventresca* or *toquilla* is the belly of the tuna and the tastiest part of the animal due to its high fat content. The most sought-after part of the animal is the roe. Each tuna has two roes. Those of the male are unsuitable for salting and are eaten fresh as an appetizer. The roes of the female, called *de grano*, have a cylindrical form when recently extracted. Once salted and dried, first in the sun and then in the dryer, it constitutes a more select and appreciated delicacy.

Other popular salted food is obtained from the shark, mackerel tuna, the *mussola* (dogfish), mackerel, salted sardine or the poor cod.

On the left. tunas in salt. Above,
learning to differentiate traditionally-made quality salted fish.

valencian_cuisine

The geography of the *coca* flat breads

The history of *cocas* in the Mediterranean basin is as old as bread or ground wheat. Greek warriors prepared them and dressed them with olives or with heated olive juice. In Rome, according to Virgil, it was popular to eat *moretum*, *coca* prepared with flour and yeast that was accompanied by onion, garlic, oil and vinegar. Some experts state that, in its origin, the *cocas* had to be circular and inevitably had a circle in the centre, possibly as a reminiscence of some ancestral solar ritual… There are theories, like *cocas*, for all tastes.

The fact is that *cocas* are deeply rooted in the gastronomic heritage of the Valencia Community. Each town, and even each family, jealously guards the secrets of the preparation of a *coca*

The art of preparing *cocas*, sweet or savoury, is deeply rooted in the homes of Valencia.

valencian_cuisine

Above, preparing a herring *coca* de arenque.

that they consider their own. All similar, all different. Sweet or savoury, flat or covered (*fassides*) but invariably delicious.

The base is always the same: a dough prepared with flour (wheat or maize), water, oil or beer, in some cases yeast or a pinch of bicarbonate of soda, and a pinch of salt or sugar. Of course, they can also have butter, white wine, muscatel, aniseed or any other spirit or spice to give them a touch of flavour. From the base, the fermentations, forms and cooking may be very different.

The range of ingredients of the different fillings is almost infinite, although, in the case of savoury *cocas* it is popular to have them with cured meats (long pork sausage, black pudding, *blanquets*, Majorcan sausage) and, above all, the more Mediterranean vegetables, such as peppers, aubergines, tomatoes, onions, artichokes, peas, Swiss chard…

The geography of the *coca* takes us to the most hidden-away corners to always surprise us with a different local traditional speciality.

Thus, the *cocas* in the Maestrat have the name of *cocs* (very popular the *coc en tomata* of Morella, *en carne magra* or *coc en sardina*). In Safor they make *coques fregides, de casa con forat al mig i sense, filaneres*… Special mention should be made of the *coques escaldades* or *a la calfó*, so popular in Oliva.

In the Alicante counties, just as one would expect, fillings with diverse salted fish are very popular. The *minxos*, thin and long *cocas*, and the *coca de molletes* are very popular indeed.

In the sweet *cocas* section we must highlight the ever-present *coca llanda* or *coca boba*, the

coques de cacau, —to which peanut is added, very popular in the counties close to Valencia—, the thin *coca* of Sant Antoni, present in many counties of the Community but originating from Alt Maestrat —such as the *coca malfeta*, the *coca celestial* ot the *coca amb molla*—, the *fogassetes* from Algemessí, the *Coca de Sant Joan*, the *coques fines*, the *coquetes a l'arrop*…

The list, both in sweet and savoury *cocas*, could fill the pages of an entire specialised encyclopaedia. In any case, it is still surprising that, in a society in which the delicious local *cocas* have always been present, the tyranny of the more common-or-garden pizzas and *focaccias* has been so clearly imposed… Paradoxes of globalisation.

Coca from Castellón, made with potato. On the left, the delicious Cristina coca or cake, based on ground almonds.

valencian_cuisine

Mediterranean cheeses

For its historic importance, the Tronchón occupies first position among the cheeses of the Valencia Community. The most famous bibliographical references that document the existence of Tronchón is the praise of its virtues that Sancho Panza makes in Don Quixote. The production zone of the Tronchón was historically extended throughout the Maestrat and Els Ports de Morella and Beceite, from the Plana de Castellón and the Delta de l'Ebre to the interior of Teruel. The cheese was made with milk from the flocks of sheep, —in which also browsed a few goats— which undertook the transhumance in the high pastureland of the Levantine sierras.

The moulds used, of olive or boxwood, had a small cone at the base to help in the exuding of the whey and give the moulded curd its characteristic form of a volcano. The shepherds of the zone chiselled out the interior of these moulds with their knives, decorating them with floral or religious motifs that remained engraved on the cheese rind.

1. Cured cloth mould cheese. **2.** Tronchón.
3. Cheese from La Nucía. **4.** Cloth cheese (*tovalló*).
5. Cassoleta. **6.** Brull.

The small and inviting *cassoleta* cheeses —which means small pan in Valencian— are in reality small Tronchòns that are traditionally made in the coastal areas with goat's milk, and sometimes a little sheep's milk, to be sold fresh or aired. Unlike that of the Tronchón, the rind of these cheeses is not engraved and it is smaller, between 100 and 150 grams. In the past they also made the *formatges de duro* or *de berenar* —snack cheeses (*berenar*) the size of a coin (*duro*)— which hardly weigh 50 grams per piece.

The cheeses of the Valencia Community are distinguished by their clear Mediterranean character and the originality of their formats.

Also of great popularity are the cloth mould cheeses (*formatges de tovalló*), fresh goat's milk cheeses that the goatherds traditionally made themselves, letting the curd rinse in a tied cloth and later submerging the pieces in a brine bath. Its preparation is very common in the Valencia county of La Costera de Ranes (Llosa de Ranes, Llanera de Ranes, Rotglà and Corbera…) and in Alicante's Alt Vinalopó (Campo de Mirra, Benejama, Vilena…). Also very popular in this zone are the fresh goat's cheeses known as *blanquets* or Alicante cheeses, moulded in esparto grass belts which leave their characteristic mark on the side of the pieces.

In the town of La Nucía, in Marina Baixa, the star of the local gastronomy is the cheese that carries the name of the town and which originated here in a very original way. The cheese of La Nucía was created by Juan Ferrer, who had the idea of making fresh goat's cheese in his own butcher's shop, adding some cow's milk and using metallic egg boxes as mould to rinse the curds. The result was surprising. The cheeses acquired a curious trunk-like conical form and an original decoration with the side markings of the diamond shape of the egg boxes. This speciality became very popular in the whole area and took the name of "cheese of La Nucía". In 1960 the Ferrer family created their own brand to sell the original cheese of La Nucía, as well as other traditional varieties: *cassoleta*, cloth mould, *puçol* and *blanquet*.

In the town of Catí, —in the centre of the valley of the mountainous area of Alicante that joins Els Ports de Morella with the hills of Maestrat— are found some of the most interesting cheeses in the whole Valencia Community. Since the late 1990s the cooperative of Catí has been committed to making quality cheeses for the most demanding palates and to constant improvement, in both structures and innovation and training. Their cheeses have obtained some of the most important prizes from the international cheese-making world. Moreover, in Morella they have another cheese dairy and with an educational information space about the rural culture of the area: the Shepherd's Museum.

Traditional cured meats

The culture of cured meats comes from the need to make full use of the meat from the slaughter of the pig (*matança* or *porquejà*) for the whole year. Traditionally a cold day was chosen around the beginning of November or later, the whole family met and looked for an expert slaughterman and a woman skilled in removing the blood to avoid it clotting.

The men were in charge of separating the pieces: hams, shoulders, bones ... The finest parts were salted and then conserved in pickle. The women chopped up the rest of the meat to prepare the different specialities: *llonganisses*, *botifarres* or black puddings with rice o onion, *xoricets*…

The *blanquet* is a *botifarró* sausage made with streaky meat and head. The Easter long sausage is traditionally made in the Valencia area. It is a very dry and thin sausage made from lean pork, veal and lard, seasoned with pepper and aniseed. The *figatells* are a type of hamburger based on lean pork and pig liver wrapped in a membrane.

The *bufa* is wrapped in the pig's bladder. The *garró* is a variant of the *bufa* but wrapped in the skin of the knuckle, typical of Xaló (in Marina Alta in Alicante). The *poltrota* is made with cooked pork rind and bacon, pork meat and meat from the head boiled with the tongue, salt and pepper.

The *perro* includes meat from the head, bacon, pork rind and spices. The *gueña*, very typical in Requena, is made with streaky bacon and offal and seasoned with pepper, cinnamon, clove, garlic and paprika.

The local *sobrassadas* can be seasoned with a pinch of orange or pumpkin. The most famous is that of Tàrbena, a town which was repopulated with families from Mallorca after the expulsion of the converts in 1609.

The cured meats made from the slaughter of the pig are present all over the Valencia Community.

I.G.P. Embutidos de Requena

The municipal district of Requena is located 690 metres above sea level in an extensive high plain surrounded by the sierras of Negrete, Cabrillas, Malacara and Martés. The climate in this area is characterised by dryness and continental nature, with marked changes of temperature between the short summers and long, cold winters, meteorological peculiarities for the perfect maturing of cured meats.

The tripe meat tradition of the area is ancestral. The pork butchers of Requena are proud of always using the sow or castrated pig meat to thus guarantee its greater quality, of using natural tripe to improve the conservation and flavour of the cured meat and of selecting only the best spices in the market.

The I.G.P. Embutidos de Requena Regulating Council comprises twelve family businesses, all of them located in the municipal district of Requena. The quality labels of the Regulating Council ensure the quality and authenticity of the product.

1 Orza: Cured meat (long sausage, chorizo or black pudding) conserved in olive oil in glazed vessels of ceramic, tall and without handles, for its annual consumption. They also conserve pork shoulder and ribs in "orza".

2 Salami sausage: Mixture of lean pork meat (80-90%) and streaky bacon (20-10%) with salt and spices (pepper and ground pepper). Minimum curing time of 18 days.

3 Sobrasada: Raw cured meat made exclusively with lean pork meat (15-20%) and bacon/streaky bacon (80-85%), with salt, spices and condiments.

4 Cured chorizo: Mixture of lean pork meat (60-70%) and bacon (40-30%), with salt and spices (paprika, pepper, garlic, cinnamon and clove) and condiments (wines and spirits).

5 & 6 Perro: Mixture of lean pork meat (15-20%) and bacon/streaky bacon (80-85%), with salt, spices (pepper, paprika and garlic) and condiments. The curing time depends on the format; thick, from 7 to 10 days, thin, from 3 to 4 days.

7 & 8 Black puddings: Mixture of cooked onion, rice (5%), lard (10-20%) and pig's blood (10-15%), with salt and spices (cinnamon, clove and pepper). They are blanched for 1 hour.

9 Fresh chorizo: It is presented as a long sausage with a more or less thin format.

10 Gueña: Mixture of streaky bacon (60-70%), offal (30-40%), previously cooked or hardened, salt, spices (pepper, paprika, cinnamon, clove and garlic) and condiments.

11 Lean: Pork meat (70-80%), bacon/streaky bacon (20-30%), salt and spices. It is presented in strings. It may be thick or thin.

The truffle of the Maestrat and Els Ports

In the lands of Maestrat and Els Ports the black truffles (*Tuber melanosporum*) are traditionally known as *pataques negres* (black potatoes). If someone found a truffle by chance in the mountain, they would throw it away for its strong smell or feed it to the pigs. The legend goes that in the nineteen-fifties "strange" French hunters appeared in the winter with a dog instead of a shotgun who collected the "black potatoes". Thus the locals learnt the value of their truffles. Their unregulated picking is done between November and February. There are a few truffle plantations established from mycorrhized holm-oaks. Every year diverse shows and gastronomic days are held. The truffle market of Morella is held with full discretion on Friday evenings close to the Portal de Sant Mateu.

Demetrio Ferrando reveals to us the secrets of picking truffles with a dog in the mountains of Benassal, in Alt Maestrat.

Stews, broths and gazpachos

The varied list of spoon-stirred stews of the Valencia Community is enormous and responds to an ancestral tradition of preparations that make full use of the market garden and the products from the sea and mountain. The result is an almost infinite catalogue, a traditional gastronomic heritage of an enormous richness that possesses all kinds of specialities and imaginative variations throughout the region of Valencia. Without the slightest doubt, the stew is the most popular spoon-stirred recipe throughout the Valencia Community.

As the gastronome Lorenzo Millo points out, it is an obligatory meal once a week in many homes and its main vegetable are cardoons. The stew is different from the broth in a main ingredient: the kidney beans or *fesols*.

Stews are a winter dish par excellence. In their composition appear the most diverse seasonal vegetables combined with rice, kidney beans or chopped wheat. The meats can also be very varied, generally veal and pork (head, trotters, hooves, cheek, ribs, bacon…) and cured meats of all types. The key: prolonged cooking for two or three hours on a very low flame to make sure the pulse is fleshy and that the stock is thick and almost gelatinised by the collagen of the meats. A warming and nutritive dish, ideal for bravely facing the cold winter days in the country.

The geography of Valencia's stews with all their variants extends from Morella to Orihuela: the *recapte* stew with jerked beef, the *benicarlanda* stew, the *segorbina* stew, the Sant Blai stew… the stew of La Plana is the fasting stew, since it has no meat. The *churra* stew, typical of Los Serranos, is made with cardoon leaves, Swiss chard, bacon, snout, backbone, bread black pudding and lamb.

The numerous local varieties of stews and broths compete with the rice dishes in importance.

Above, detail of flat bread for gazpachos.

There are stews for all tastes; gypsy stews, soldier's stews, notary stews… One of the most famous recipes is the musician's stew, very popular in Alcoy. They say that the recipe was prepared without rice so that the musicians who enlivened the festivals of Moors and Christians could eat it after playing and so the rice would not have been overcooked.

Until being dethroned by the paella, the broth was the unarguable king of Valencia gastronomy, the dish of festivals and Christmas, when rural families sacrificed their meat reserves —a turkey or a hen fed over a period of several months— to prepare a special meal in which they did not skimp on either quantities or ingredients. The Sunday broths were more modest but the approach was the same: one day the broth is made and the following days the leftovers are used for a rice dish or simply sautéing them with tomatoes and fried garlic.

First the soup is served with a *pilota* (meatball) and later the chickpeas are served in a bowl with the vegetables (potatoes, turnips, cabbage, parsnip, yam…); in another bowl is served the bacon (*garreta*), the bones, the *blanquets*, the chorizo and the remaining *pilotes*; and in a third bowl are served the pieces of chicken and hen.

The *pilotes* —also called *fassedures*, *rellenos* or *tarongetes*— are meatballs the size of an orange. They are made with mincemeat, breadcrumbs and egg, although the most diverse ingredients and spices may form part of their preparation: pine nuts, parsley, milk, clove, nutmeg, blood, chicken liver, grated lemon peel… In Marina Baixa and La Ribera they are sometimes wrapped in cabbage leaves and in other places are called *bordes* and have bullet salted tuna or *sangatxo* added. They can also be made with corn flour (*farcedures de panís* or *dacsa*) or sweetened in flavour with sugar, cinnamon, yam and almond flour.

Among many other singular broths we would mention the *pava borracha*, typical of Vega Baja and the octopus broth, very popular in Calp, Benissa and Moraira.

Although little is known of their origin, the gazpachos belong to a very old and pastoral culture, very possibly prior to the arrival of the Roman legions to the peninsula. For those not versed in gastronomic affairs, we should point out that these gazpachos have nothing whatsoever in common with the famous Andalusian gazpacho, a liquid obtained from blended vegetables. The Valencia mountain gazpachos are made with game meat or poultry, seasoned with wild herbs and served mandatorily with flat or unleavened breads.

The flat bread was once kneaded on a goatskin and flattened until it was very thin so that it's cooking would be uniform once covered by the embers. Then it was turned over and cooked on the other side. As Francisco G. Seijo Alonso stated, the flat bread is "the soul of the gazpacho" and without doubt makes up the most characteristic element of the dish. In some places, the gazpacho is served over the flat bread, used as a plate; on other occasions they serve the flat bread and the meat separately; finally, in the most

Details of the traditional preparation of the gazpacho.
Below, leaves of pebrella or thyme (*Thymus pyperella*).

valencian_cuisine

popular version, the flat bread is chopped up and served mixed with the gazpacho.

The gazpachos are traditionally prepared with game meat of either fur or feather: rabbit, hare, partridge or wood pigeon. Today they are also made with farm poultry and some creative chefs have even popularised marine gazpachos, with grouper, tuna, calamari, Dublin Bay prawns and prawns. The wild herbs that are used are the *pebrella* (*Thymus pyperella*), oregano, mint and laurel.

In the villages around Macizo del Caroig and in the Alicante valleys of the River Vinalopó, the gazpachos form an authentic sign of identity and attract a multitude of visitors who come to taste the ancestral speciality.

Eating a perfect gazpacho in the legendary Mesón El Viscayo, in Castalla. On the right, flat bread with gazpacho.

valencian_cuisine

Albufera: hunting and fishing

The Natural Park of the Albufera is a series of humid coastal ecosystems —lake, mud bank and marshland— located to the south of the city of Valencia. The rivers Túria, in the north, and Xúquer, in the south, supply the water needs of the crops and border the park, also framed by two natural elevations of the Iberian system: the Perenxissa and Corbera sierras.

The lake of Albufera is the largest on the Iberian peninsula, with 2,837 hectares. In winter, the sluices of the artificial canals are closed and the park is flooded to create the "game reserves" and for sowing the rice, a single crop farming area that currently covers 14,000 hectares, represent-

Above, fishermen at work. On the right, idyllic corner of the Valencia Albufera during the first light of the morning.

ing 70% of the extension of the lagoon. Other crops of less importance are the orange groves and vegetables.

Traditionally the lagoon has been a privileged spot for hunting. In 1987, a year after the establishment of the Natural Park, hunting was banned in the lake except for the annual shoots in the reserves of Sueca, Cullera and Silla. Eight shoots are made in the season every Saturday, between the end of November and mid-January.

After the auction of the game reserves, the wooden barrels (*bocois*) or wattle stockades are placed in which the hunters hide, organise surveillance and close the entrances so that the birds are not disturbed.

The marshland area occupied by game reserves currently extends for more than 13,000 hectares, of which some 4,000 correspond to "reserves". The most sought-after species in Sueca and Cullera are the northern pintail and the red-crested pochard. In Silla, the main specie is the coot.

Fishing was historically the greatest wealth in the area until, in the 18th century, agricultural use began to gain importance and weaken the fishing exploitation, basically due to the silting of the lake to gain rice cultivation.

Two moments of eel fishing.

Until a few decades ago, eels and sea bass were the specie of most importance within the local economy. The eel is the main ingredient in the most emblematic dishes of gastronomy in the area: the *all i pebre*. The most appreciated variety and of the most delicate meat is the *maresa* eel, with a white belly and blue back.

Nevertheless, today mullet and carp are much more abundant. Other outstanding species are the *gavatxa* prawn (*Dugastella valentina*), endemic to the Valencia region and the freshwater shrimp (*Palaemonetes zariquieyi*). The American red crab, detested for the damage it causes to the rice fields and other endemic species, was introduced during the nineteen-seventies to be bred artificially.

Among the species of threatened fish feature the Valencia toothcarp or *samaruc* (*Valencia hispanica*), the Spanish toothcarp or *fartet* (*Aphanius iberus*) and the *raboseta* (*Cobitis paludica*), a type of sardine.

The municipalities of the Natural Park of the Albufera of Valencia belong to four counties: Ribera Alta, Ribera Baixa, Horta Sud and Ciutat de València.

valencian_cuisine

As a gastronomic curiosity we should mention the water rat or *talpó*, which traditionally was highly appreciated for its culinary value. Thus, we read in Vicente Blasco Ibáñez in his entertaining novel "*Cañas y Barro*": "The marshland rats only ate rice, they were food fit for a king. There was nothing else but to see them in the market in Sueca (…) The wealthy bought them; the aristocracy of the towns of La Ribera did not eat anything else". Today, due to the use of pesticides in rice-growing, it is not recommended to eat them.

The biodiversity and ecological importance of this marvellous natural space is seriously threatened by factors of the most diverse type. The interests and opinions of the different groups linked to the Natural Park are many and, sometimes, in conflict. Diverse associations work very hard to conciliate positions through dialogue trying to promote political decisions regarding ecological and environmental protection.

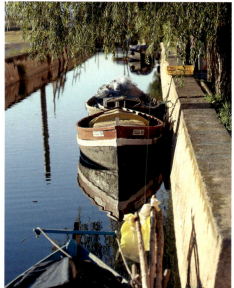

On the left, returning from fishing. On the right, detail of the Irrigation channels and canals that provide the watering of the orchards and rice fields.

Sweet temptations

1 *Pastel de Gloria*
The cake base, a crunchy wafer biscuit covered with a layer of egg yolk and sugar topping, is called "hell" and supports the lightness of the merengue in the form of a cone pointing up towards the sky which, of course, is "glory". It may have other more mundane names such as "cow's udder" or "nun's nipple". In Xixona they call the tartlets of Gloria balls of marzipan filled with sweet potato and coated in icing sugar.

2 Toñas
The same dough for similar recipes with different names: *toñas, panquemaos, panous, micos, cócs, fogassas, manojoias.* The secret consists of leaving the dough to rest for some hours so that it ferments slowly and acquires the delicate texture of brioche that characterises them. They are typical in several counties at Easter and for preparing the *monas*, Easter cakes.

3 *Oropesinas*
A creation with an almond base from the cake-makers Ismael Requena and Bruno Forner to boost the promotion of tourism In Oropesa in the 1980s. They are inspired by the traditional cake-making of the area and have become an authentic gastronomic reference of the town.

4 *Monas*
The origin of the Easter *mona* could be In the Roman rituals that were held in honour of the goddess Ceres when spring began. The *mona* is a sweet bun, In the form of a ring or a long strip, sugared on top and with a hard-boiled egg In the centre. The egg is the symbol of life that is reborn after the winter. It is eaten on trips to the countryside on Easter Sunday and Monday, the festival of San Vicente Ferrer and the annual procession of Santa Faz.

valencian_cuisine

5 *Arrop* and *tallaetes*
The *arrop* is made by boiling grape juice until obtaining a type of thick dark syrup. The *tallaetes* are thin slices of pumpkin, although they are also sometimes made with plums, peaches and even with thins strips of the white part of watermelon skin.

6 Fritters
During the *fallas* festival, Valencia smells of gunpowder and fritters. The city is filled with open-air stands in the street where they fry and sell fritters made with pumpkin, figs.
The tradition of fritters is widespread throughout the Valencia Community and some say "that there is no festival without *bunyols*".

7 *Flaons de brull*
Sweet pastries made with a dough aromatised with aniseed and filled with a mixture of cottage cheese, ground almond and cinnamon. They are baked until golden and served well sprinkled with a mixture of sugar and cinnamon. Essential for sweetening any visit to the towns of Els Ports and, of course, Morella.

8 *Almoixàvena*
Moixavena, monjávena, almoixavena, almojábana... There are as many names as there are variants of this typical recipe of Arab origin. The irreplaceable ingredient is the pork lard which, without the slightest doubt, is the Christian contribution that could never have been In the original recipe... It is typical in Xàtiva and Ontinyent during Lent and on All Saints Day.

9 **Arnadí**
Although it can be found easily throughout the year, *arnadí* is a sweet typical at Easter. Like many other cake-making preparations in the Valencia Community it is of Arab origin. It can be made with pumpkin or yam, or with a mixture of both. The exterior decorations, based on peeled almonds, may be very diverse depending on the aesthetic tastes of each.

10 *Fartons*
In the 1960s the Polo family settled in Alboraya and decided to create a new product with a special texture that could be dipped into the horchata drink, tiger nut milk, absorbing the liquid without crumbling up. Thus were born the now popular *fartons*. They are lengthened buns lightly covered with icing sugar, ideal for dipping into the horchata and other hot drinks, such as drinking chocolate or coffee.

Nougat from Xixona and Alicante

Turrón, nougat, is of Arab origin. There are historical data conserved about the manufacture of nougat in the 16th century in the city of Sexona, later Xixona or Jijona.

The great expansion of the nougat market took place after the Civil War, with the emigration across Spain of republican workers from Alicante who ended up opening many ice cream and *turrón* parlours around the country.

The Marcona almond is the authentic base of the nougat along with other local varieties admitted by the Regulating Council such as the valencia, mallorca, mollar, planeta and llargueta. Industrially other almonds of diverse origin are used that are less flavoursome.

The honey used must be pure bees' honey of the mil flores, rosemary, saffron or other single flower varieties from Alicante, Valencia or Castellón.

The Regulating Council guarantees minimum percentages of 10% pure bees' honey and

a quantity of almond of 52% for the Xixona and 46% for the nougat from Alicante.

The nougats protected by the Designation of Origin Xixona and Turrón de Alicante have two labels that differentiate the qualities: Suprema (gold) and Extra (silver) according to the percentage of almond used in their elaboration: 64% and 50% respectively for the Xixona and 60% and 46% for the Turrón de Alicante.

On being a very seasonal product, during the rest of the year the workers of Xixona usually work producing other food products, generally ice creams, sugared almonds, glazed fruits or shortbreads.

The nougats linked to the most ancestral elaboration are those from Xixona, Alicante and the tortas of Alicante.

valencian_cuisine

Turrón de Xixona

The artisanal method of making nougat is still the same as the traditional method carried out for hundreds of years.

1 The dough of the nougat is made by cooking the honey with peeled and toasted almond, sugars and egg white. The master nougat maker takes a little dough, called "the wire", stretches it forming a thread, rolls it, and tests it by seeing if it crunches between his teeth. If this is the case, it is ready. Later, the peeled and toasted almond is added, mixing it manually with the heated dough with the aid of some wooden sticks in the form of oars (the *punxes*).

2 & 3 The dough is then spread on special tables so that it cools and then put into granite mills to grind it.

4 The resulting mass is then passed through a refiner to a achieve the desired texture.
5 After this process it is subjected to a second heating in the recipient called a *boixet* for a minimum of 150 minutes in order to compact the mass.
6 & 7 The final process is known as "completion". The mass is taken from the *Boixet* and placed in moulds and then left to rest for a minimum of 48 hours before the cutting and packing processes.

valencian_cuisine

Turrón de Alicante

The elaboration of nougat from Alicante is similar to the above, but at the end of the process diluted egg white is added.

1 & 2 The process begins in the same way as the nougat from Xixona. In a rotating mixer called "mechanical", with a capacity of 50 to 60 kg a mixture of sugar and honey is heated on a very low flame The peeled almond is toasted in rotating cylinders ("toasters") heated on a high flame and then added to the mixture. Then diluted egg white is added as a whitener to acwhitener, until achieving, by evaporation, the "tip of the ball" necessary..

3 The mass is stirred manually with the punxes (sticks in the form of oars) to mix it in a uniform way.

4 & 5 Then, still hot, the mass is weighed and moulded in boxes covered with wafers, of 6 kg capacity.

valencian_cuisine

Land of ice creams

At the end of the 19th century, many ice cream sellers from the Alicante towns of Ibi and Xixona began to move towards the big cities in the countries to sell their ice creams in summer and the nougat in the Christmas period. In the nineteen-twenties the challenge was even greater: many families decided to cross the pond to establish their businesses in Cuba, Argentina and Mexico. Others settled in the Canaries, Morocco and Algeria.

After the Spanish Civil War, this diaspora would be caused by force majeure: those ice cream sellers who had fought for the republic and over whose heads hung prison sentences, or execution, found in their itinerant trade the pretext to distance themselves from the towns in which they would be easily found.

In 1958 the first technical-health legislation regarding ice cream was passed and many of these families began to open fixed establishments in order to be able to work complying with the demands of the new regulations. Numerous establishments that were opened during these years across Spain have survived until today.

The families from Ibi and Xixona meet after Christmas and until March, when they reopen their ice cream parlours. This is why the Moors and Christians festivals are held here in February, with the emotive offerings of the ice cream sellers attractively adorned with the regional costumes of the different communities where they run their establishments.

The ice creams made in the Alicante towns of Ibi and Xixona are famous all over Spain.

valencian_cuisine

The tiger nut and the horchata drink

Local gastronomic legends say that in the tombs of the Egyptians pharaohs millenary amphorae have been found containing tiger nuts, such was the love of the ancient civilisations for this small fleshy tuber to which miraculous properties were attributed. Without doubt, drinking lovely fresh tiger nut milk, *horchata,* on a hot summer's day is still a prodigious remedy that cures all ills…

Tiger nuts are the underground tubers produced by the roots of a species of sedge, a cyperaceae plant called tiger nut sedge. Its scientific name is *Cyperus Esculentus*. The plant can reach up to 40 cm in height.

The tiger nut is the edible part and can be eaten raw, cooked or in flour. As well as its use in making the delicious *horchata*, quality oil can be extracted from it.

In the 7th century the Arabs introduced its cultivation into the Mediterranean area. Today, the tiger nut with the D.O. Valencia is grown in sixteen towns in the county of L'Horta del Nord. Here they produce some 5.3 million kilos annually, of which 90% are protected by the Designation of Origin. The suitability of the cultivation area lies in a climate with abundant humidity, medium-high temperatures and loose soils, well levelled and drained, and just above sea level.

Sowing the tiger nut takes place between April and May, depending on the previous harvest.

Harvesting is done with a combine harvester when the plant is completely dry and withered,

Tiger nut milk with fartons. On the right, detail of clean and dry tiger nuts.

between November and January. Washing is then carried out to remove the impurities. The tubers are then placed in layers of 10-20 cm and stirred once or twice a day so that they dry well for three months before selecting and washing them again. The tiger nuts, now clean and dry, are classified by calibre before packing.

The most common types of tiger nut are rounded and long, known in Valencia as *llargueta* (long) and *armela* (rounded).

Selection process of tiger nuts before packing to remove impurities and classify them according to their calibre.

To make a good *horchata* you need 500 g of tiger nuts, 200 g of brown sugar, a cinnamon stick, the peel of a small lemon and two litres of water. The tiger nuts must be left previously to soak in water for 12 hours (if left for more time, they lose flavour). Then they are washed, rinsed and mashed in a mixer or a kitchen blender with two litres of water. Pour the mixture into a recipient, add the sugar, cinnamon and lemon peel and leave to rest for 4 hours. Then sieve the mixture with a cloth strainer and squeeze it well.

The juice that comes out is the *horchata*, which is cooled in the fridge stirring it every hour so that it does not solidify. When serving, it is a good idea to accompany it with the typical *fartons*, long buns with icing, which convert the tasting into an almost mystical experience.

Drying the tiger nuts is done in *cambres* for a period of three months. They are stirred twice a day.

Wines and spirits: millenary tradition

Neolithic archaeological digs document the existence of grapes in the Mediterranean Levant from ancient antiquity. The Phoenicians developed cuttings of muscatel from Alexandria, a variety of grape that would adapt admirably to the lands of Alicante. In the 1st century BC the wine of Sagunto, which would become very popular in the Middle Ages, already appears mentioned in the texts of Juvenal and Martial. The Romans developed a parallel industry to manufacture the amphorae necessary for exporting and selling the wines of the area around the Mediterranean, using the privileged location that the large maritime ports provided.

In the mid-19th century, the successive waves of phylloxera in France meant an increase in production of wine in bulk. In the 1970s and 1980s the port of Valencia exported millions of litres of wine in bulk produced not only in the Valencia Community but also Catalonia, Murcia, Castile and Aragon.

The wine in bulk crisis and the emergence of wines from the New World acted as a major reagent that would trigger off the renovation and modernisation of the sector. With an eye on the international markets, which in those years the single-variety wines flourished, they began to introduce the more world-famous varieties (Cabernet Sauvignon, Merlot, Chardonnay…) or at a national level (Tempranillo, Macabeo…). With time the autochthonous varieties (Monastrell, Bobal…) once again took on a leading role and the recovery of other varieties which had been practically forgotten (Tardana, Mandó…). The cellars were modernised with big investments and it did not take long before there were results.

The modernisation of the cellars, adaptation to new varieties of grape and the recovery of autochthonous stocks define a sector in constant evolution.

valencian_cuisine

Above, an aspect of the grape harvest. On the right, detail of the carts used traditionally in Utiel to transport the grapes and wineskins of wine.

The geography of the wines of the Valencia Community covers an extensive area with great diversity of climate, soils and varieties.

The Valencia Designation of Origin is divided into four regions: Alto Turia, Clariano, Moscatel de Valencia and Valentino. Due to the excellent geographic location and the warm climate, here are produced the red wines with most colour in the Spanish Levant. Also produced are sweet whites, rosés, sparkling liqueurs, sparkling aromatic and mellowed wines.

Some of the large producers, located traditionally close to the port, relocated further inland in the years of the city's restructuring, building new and modern installations closer to the cultivated land.

The Utiel-Requena Designation of Origin has the most extensive area of vineyards in the Valencia Community. Geographically it is situated between the two rivers of southeast Valencia, the Turia and the Cabriel, and has quite a gentle orography, with rolling hills and soils with a high lime content. It takes in the wines produced in the municipal districts of Camporrobles, Caudete de Las Fuentes, Fuenterrobles, Requena, Siete Waters, Sinarcas, Utiel, Venta del Moro and Villargordo del Cabriel. The climate of the area is continental with short, dry summers and cold, very long winters that sometimes reach extreme temperatures.

The Bobal red grape variety is by far the most grown in the area. Its existence on these lands is documented from the 15th century. In the mid-19th century, when phylloxera devastated the European vineyards, the local winemaking industry grew enormously in order to enter into external markets. In fact, the stocks of the Bobal variety showed a strong resistance to the parasite and they were able to be replanted with American grafted roots.

There are still many underground cellars of great antiquity, before the Christian occupation, which have been traditionally used to store the wine. Today we should mention the large investments made in new cellars provided with the most modern installations.

The El Terrerazo Protected Designation of Origin represents the recognition of the first wine vineyard in the Mediterranean, produced in this estate of Utiel.

The old winemaking tradition of the province of Alicante experienced its age of splendour during the 16th and 17th centuries. After a long and dark period for winemaking in these estates, which coincided with the Muslim occupation and the years after the Reconquista, a royal edict safeguarded production prohibiting wines from other areas from entering Alicante, as well as the dispatching of wines that were not from Alicante from the city port. Swedish, Flemish and English traders imported wines from the province and the city of Monóvar was famous for its prestig-

ious Fondillón. In the 19th century the prices of wine from Alicante were four or six times more than those from Jerez or Oporto. The situation was complicated when phylloxera devastated the vineyards in a particularly cruel way.

The vineyards of the Alicante Designation of Origin are divided into two quite different areas. The first is on the riverside of the River Vinalopó, which extends behind the city of Alicante, and where the Monastrell grape shares its hegemony

The Fondillón wine is made only with the Monastrell grape variety in the Alicante counties of Alto and Medio Vinalopó.

with other new varieties. The second, the area of La Marina, and much smaller, is on the north coast with a warm and humid climate, the ideal land for the Moscatel grape. Also known as Moscatel de Alejandría, Moscatel Romano or Moscatel de Alicante, this variety is greatly appreciated as both a table wine and in the preparation of sweet wines.

The Fondillón is a fine wine with an alcohol content of between 16% and 18%, generally dry, or semi-dry, which matures in old oak barrels for a period that may range from between ten and twenty years. It is a wine made with the Monastrell grape variety that reaches its high alcohol content through over-ripening on the stock itself, with a dark colour originally which becomes amber after the ageing process.

When the bottles are filled, a part of each barrel is switched to the next one, filling the loss with old wine. It is the system known as "scale of vintages".

valencian_cuisine

In his memoirs the Duke of Saint-Simon wrote that the "Sun king", Louis XIV of France, loved cakes soaked in Fondillón. It also appears mentioned in the novel "The Count of Monte Cristo" by Alexander Dumas. The count asks the Marquis of Cavalcanti, a connoisseur of the best wines, to choose between a sherry, a port or Fondillón. The marquis replies that his favourite is the Fondillón of Alicante.

The province of Castellón also has an important winemaking tradition. However, an enormous extension of vineyards was replaced mainly by citric fruit crops in the early nineteen-eighties. The areas of production are the Alto Palancia-Alto Mijares, Sant Mateu and Les Useres-Vilafamés.

Special mention should be made of the production of spirits and liqueurs, deeply rooted in the Community. In Alicante we must mention the Cantueso or Herbero from the Sierra de Mariola, made with local wild or semi-wild herbs, the Aperitivo-Café from Alcoy and the Anís Paloma from Monforte del Cid. In the small village of Xert, in the Maestrat, we find the brandy and spirits of the traditional distillery of Julián Segarra. In Benicàssim the Licor Carmelitano is typical, created by the Carmelite Fathers more than one hundred years ago in the basement of the old monastery of the Desierto de las Palmas. Much more recent are the Arancello, of Italian inspiration or the Licor de Horchata de Chufa de Valencia.

The making of spirits and liqueurs is deeply rooted in the Valencia Community.

valencian_cuisine

OTHER PRODUCTS

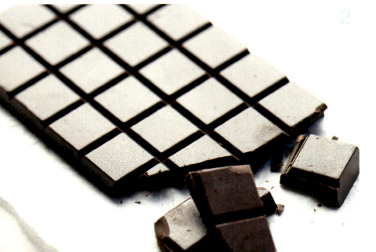

1 Olive oil
The olive tree has traditionally occupied extensive lands of the Valencia Community and the prestige of its oils is age-old. The extra virgin olive oil with Designation of Origin Aceite de Oliva de la Comunitat Valenciana is made with autochthonous varieties, some of which cannot be found in any other part of the country: Manzanilla Villalonga, Blanqueta, Farga, Serrana de Espadán, Morruda, Cornicabra, Alfafara or Grosal, Changlot Real, Rojal, Canetera, Nana, Arbequina, Empeltre, Cuquillo, Sollana, Callosina, Llumeta, Millarenca and Borriolenca. The designation has eight sub-areas: Maestrat, Plana Alta-Alacatén, Sierras de Espadán and Calderona, Serranías de Turia-Ribera del Magro, Utiel-Requena-Valle de Ayora, Macizo del Caroig-Vall de Albaida, Montaña de Alicante and Vinalopó.

2 La Vila and chocolate
It was a chocolate seller of Italian origin, in refuge in La Vila Joiosa fleeing the Napoleonic army, who in 1810 introduced the art of chocolate making in La Vila. Soon the trade of *xocolater* and the manufacture of chocolate expanded and

other families set up the first chocolate companies. During the second half of the 19th century they began to introduce the manual mills and the first mechanical processes in its elaboration. The Museum of Chocolate of the Valor factory exhibits old machinery and utensils to learn the history and manufacture of chocolate in a didactic way.

In August *Xocolatissima* is held, a gastronomic event in which they organise many tasting sessions, activities and visits to the three chocolate factories in La Vila Joiosa.

3 Saffron

It is considered the king of spices. It is an indispensable ingredient of the Valencia Community cookbook, above all in the preparation of numerous stews, rice and noodle dishes. From the mid-19th century, with the opening of the Suez Canal, saffron has been exported around the world from the town of Novelda in Alicante's Vinalopó Medio. Traditionally the saffron that is commercialised from these lands comes from crops of other communities such as La Mancha and Aragón. To recognise good-quality saffron you should check that the threads are a uniform colour and, above all, do not have a straw-like appearance that changes quickly from red to yellowy.

4 Aromatic herbs

The original use of wild and aromatic herbs in the sierras of the Valencia Community dates back to the remotest

of times. Many of these varieties have been used for medicinal purposes or as flavouring in cooking. The different spots of the Sierra de Mariola, in the north of the Alicante province, provide many aromatic herbs with which the popular Herbero de Cantueso local liqueur is made. Among its ingredients feature sage, camomile, pennyroyal, lemon verbena, St. Benedict's thistle, peppermint, fountain grass, santonica or St Blas grass, fennel, aniseed, lemon balm, agrimony, winter savory, felty germander, thyme, dittany and French lavender. Some companies and cooperatives have begun the organic cultivation of diverse species for their commercialisation.

5 Snails

Vaquetes, xonetes, moros, avellanencs... Snails arouse true passions among the people of Valencia and there is deeply-rooted culture all around. Going into the mountains and collecting them after a rainy morning is a uniquely gratifying activity comparable to the pleasure of eating them with friends in the typical *caragolás*. They are a very common ingredient in many traditional stews, *tombets*, rice dishes and paellas. A curious recipe is snails a la *barraqueta del Nano*, stewed with garlic, herbs, white wine and chopped anchovies. The name refers to a popular one-act comedy written by Paco Barchino in 1921.

6 Honey

Apiculture has been a traditional trade since time immemorial. The most diverse flowers of the hills and mountains, as well as the closeness of diverse fruit orchards, give rise

to exquisite types of pure bees' honey of diverse varieties. Moreover, honey is an indispensable ingredient in many traditional sweets, including nougat. The Valencia Community is the number one honey producer in the country with a production that represents approximately a quarter of the national total. The most representative honeys are the rosemary, orange blossom and lemon varieties. The range of honeys is completed by the almond, thyme, lavender, albaida, sunflower, French lavender, heather, mil flowers, aniseed, apple tree and medlar.

7 Raisins

The trade in raisins from the moscatel variety was traditionally an important economic activity, above all in the county of La Marina Alta. The bunches were exposed directly to the sun to obtain the "virgin raisin" or was dried after a brief scalding for a few seconds in a cauldron with boiling water, caustic soda and herbs that helped the "scalded raisins" to get colour. Later, they were placed over wattle in the *riu-raus*, typical constructions of the area, with covered porches and large arches facing the east or north. These raisins became world famous, being exported above all to England and the United States from the port of Dénia. The phylloxera crisis and later competition from the Greek Corinthian raisins, without pips, meant the decline of the sector.

valencian_cuisine

01

130_rice with parsnips and kidney beans
132_soupy rice with rabbit, saffron milk caps and vegetables
135_ship's soup
136_dirty rice
138_black rice
141_baked rice
142_rice with crust
144_rice with seafood from alicante
147_rice del *senyoret*
148_paella valenciana
150_paella alicantina
153_paella castellonense
154_seafood paella
156_cod and cauliflower paella

rice dishes

valencian_cuisine

arròs amb fesols i naps
rice with parsnips and kidney beans

for 4-6 people

* 300 g of rice D.O. Valencia * 200 g of white beans * 6 small parsnips * 400 g of beef shank * 1 trotter and 1 pig's ear * 150 g of pork chop * 2 onion black puddings * 2 *blanquets* * 1 ripe tomato * 1 teaspoon of paprika * 2 threads of saffron * salt

1. Leave the kidney beans to soak overnight. Cover them with cold water in a pot and cook them on a medium flame along with the pork chop, the ear and the trotter. Leave to cook for 2 hours or the time necessary for the kidney beans to be tender. Half way through, rectify with salt and add the chopped parsnips, *blanquets* and black puddings.
2. Meanwhile, in a pan with two spoonfuls of oil, prepare a sauce base with the peeled and chopped tomato. Season with a pinch of salt, paprika and saffron.
3. When the kidney beans are ready remove all the ingredients except the kidney beans and chop them.
4. Add the prepared sauce base, the rice and add the chopped meats and parsnips again. Continue cooking for 18 more minutes. It should be syrupy. Leave to rest a few moments and serve.

This solid winter rice dish is also known as "caldera". A few cardoon leaves can be added, previously cooked in another pot with boiling salted water. In other versions parsnips, celery, carrots (*carlotes*) or kohirabi (*napicol*) are also added.

valencian_cuisine

arròs caldós amb conill, esclata-sangs i verdures
soupy rice with rabbit, saffron milk caps and vegetables

for 4 people

* ½ rabbit * 2 artichokes * ½ red pepper * 50 g of peas * 200 g of rice * 1 ripe tomato * 1 small bunch of parsley * 250 g of Saffron milk caps * 2 cloves of garlic * saffron * olive oil * pepper * salt

1. Chop the rabbit. Clean the artichokes removing the stem, ends, the interior hay and the outer leaves. Cut them into six pieces. Clean the pepper and dry it and remove the stalk and seeds. Cut it into squares. Peel and chop the tomato. Peel and chop the cloves of garlic. Wash the parsley and chop it finely.

2. Clean the mushrooms with a clean cloth or pass them briefly under the tap to remove all the earth and chop them.

3. Heat three spoonfuls of oil in a casserole dish and cook the pieces of rabbit on all sides until they acquire a nice golden colour. Add the tomato and the peppers and cook 5 more minutes.

4. Add the Saffron milk caps and the chopped garlic, season, sprinkle abundantly with chopped parsley and cook 5 more minutes. Cover with water and bring to the boil.

5. When it has boiled, add the rice, the artichokes and the peas. Rectify with seasoning, add the saffron and leave to cook on a medium flame for 18 minutes. It should be soupy.

You can replace the Saffron milk caps for any other fresh mushroom in season.

caldero de barca
ship's soup

for 4 people

* 400 g of rice * 400 g of conger eel * 450 g of greater weever or other rock fish
* 450 g of stargazer or other rock fish * 1 mackerel * 1 tomato * 2 ñoras * 4 cloves of garlic
* saffron * olive oil * salt

1. Heat three spoonfuls of oil in a casserole or in an iron pot and sauté the ñoras, peeled garlic cloves and chopped tomato. Remove and crush them in a mortar along with a pinch of saffron and a pinch of salt.

2. In the same oil, sauté in turns the fish with the firmest meat (stargazer, greater weever and conger eel), having previously cut them into thick slices and seasoned them. Also sauté the mackerel and put aside.

3. Add the fish to the pot again (except the mackerel), cover with water and leave to cook for 20 minutes. After 10 minutes of cooking, add the mackerel.

4. Drain the fish carefully and put them to one side on a source of heat. Strain the stock.

5. Lightly sauté the rice in a paella pan or in the same pot with three spoonfuls of oil. Add the crushed sauce base, stir and pour in the fish stock nice and hot. Rectify with salt if necessary and leave to cook for 18 minutes.

6. Serve the rice as a first course, and then the tray of fish accompanied, if you like, by some alioli or salmorreta sauce.

Traditionally, on the boats the fish was eaten first to avoid it getting cold and then the rice was prepared. These fishermen's soups can include any type of fish. In Villajoyosa or Torrevieja the soups may contain monkfish, skate, redfish, calamari or octopus. Some liver is also added to the crushed sauce base before sautéing with the garlic and ñoras.

valencian_cuisine

arròs brut
dirty rice

para 4 personas

* 400 g of rice * 230 of spinach * 400 g of tender broad beans * 4 artichokes * 125 g of tender *garrofó* * 8 young garlics * 2 tomatoes * ½ spoonful of sweet paprika * ½ lemon * saffron * olive oil * pepper * salt

1. Clean the artichokes removing the stem, ends, outer leaves and interior hay. Cut them into six pieces and leave them in a bowl with water and half a squeezed lemon to avoid them blackening.

2. Clean the spinach, remove the roots, wash them under a jet of water and leave them to drain. Shell the broad beans. Clean the young garlics and slice them. Peel the tomatoes, remove the pips and chop them.

3. Heat four spoonfuls of oil in a casserole dish and sauté the young garlics for 4 minutes. Add the chopped tomato, spinach, artichokes and broad beans, season and sauté for 5 more minutes.

4. Add the *garrofó*, paprika and pour the hot water (calculate four parts water for one of rice), season and bring to the boil. Leave this stock to reduce a few minutes and add the rice and saffron.

5. Cook for 18 minutes and leave for a few minutes to rest before serving. It should be syrupy.

Typical of Ribera Baixa, this delicious syrupy rice gets its unusual name from the dark colour that the stock of artichokes and vegetables from the Ribera del Xùquer give it.

valencian_cuisine

arròs negre
black rice

para 4 personas

* 400 g of rice * 1 half cuttlefish * 250 g of prawns * 1 onion * 2 tomatoes * 1 ñora
* 2 cloves of garlic * 1 small bunch of parsley * 1 morrón pepper * 1 small glass of white wine
* 1 laurel leaf * 800 g of small fish or stock fish * salt

1. Peel and chop the onion. Peel the cloves of garlic. Wash the pepper, remove the stem and the inner seeds and cut them into squares. Peel the tomato, remove the pips and chop it. Chop the parsley finely.

2. Clean the cuttlefish removing the beak, the eyes, the mantle and the guts. Keep the sac of ink to one side. Chop the tentacles and cut the body and fins into squares.

3. Clean all the fish for the stock and place it in a casserole dish. Cover with 3 litres of water, salt it, add a laurel leaf and bring to the boil. Leave to reduce for 30 minutes on a medium flame. Leave to rest and drain.

4. Heat four spoonfuls of oil in a casserole dish and sauté the prawns for 30 seconds. Remove them and put to one side. In the same oil briefly fry the ñora and the cloves of garlic whole. Remove them and crush them in a mortar along with the tomato and parsley.

5. In the same oil, sauté the onion on a low flame for 10 minutes. Add the chopped cuttlefish and the squares of red pepper and sauté for 4 more minutes. Pour in the white wine, leave it to reduce a few moments on a high flame and add the tomato. Season with salt and add the base in the mortar and the sac of ink diluted in some spoonfuls of stock. Cook 2 more minutes.

6. Add the rice, sauté a few moments and cover with the hot fish stock (calculate double the stock than the rice and then a bit more). Cook firstly for 10 minutes on a high flame and then 8 more minutes on a low flame. Add the prawns again when half cooked. It should be rather syrupy.

The black rice can be prepared syrupy, soupy or also dry in a paella pan. It can be served accompanied by *allioli*.

arròs al forn
baked rice

for 4 people

* 400 g of rice * 400 g of chopped rib * 200 g of chopped bacon * 100 g of dry chick peas or 200 g of cooked chick peas * 3 tomatoes * 1 potato * 1 whole garlic * 2 onion black puddings * some threads of saffron * 1 dl of olive oil * salt

1. Leave the chick peas to soak overnight covered with water. Peel the potato and cut it into fine strips. Grate the tomato.
2. Cook the chick peas in a casserole dish with lots of water until they are tender. Drain and put them to one side.
3. Fry the grated tomato lightly on a low flame in a casserole dish with the oil for 10 minutes. Add the chopped meats (except the black puddings) and sauté them until they are sealed.
4. Add the drained chick peas. Season with salt and some threads of saffron and cover generously with water. Bring to the boil and cook for 50 minutes, adding more water if necessary.
5. In a casserole dish with a flat base add the rice. Pour in 750 ml of the stock obtained and all the contents of the casserole dish.
6. Decorate with the slices of potato and the black puddings split in two. Place the whole garlic in the centre, taking away the outer skins until seeing the cloves and ensure that it is submerged in the stock. Cook in an oven preheated at 250° C for 25 minutes. Leave to rest a few minutes outside the oven and serve.

To save time you can prepare the stock with the meats in a pressure cooker. In this case, calculate about 15 minutes from when the valve is closed.
In season you can add chopped cardoon leaves to the stock.

valencian_cuisine

arròs amb crosta
rice with crust

for 4 people

* 400 g of rice * 2 onion black puddings * 300 g of bacon * 2 chicken legs * 200 g of cooked chick peas * 4 cloves of garlic * 3 tomatoes * 6 eggs * some threads of saffron * 1 dl of olive oil * salt

1. Grate the tomato. Peel and chop the cloves of garlic.
2. Heat the oil in a casserole dish and sauté the grated tomato with the crushed garlics on a low flame for 10 minutes. Add the chicken legs and the chopped bacon and cook 5 more minutes.
3. Season with salt and some threads of saffron and cover generously with water. Bring to the boil and leave to cook for 50 minutes, adding more water if necessary.
4. Pre-heat the oven at 250° C. Debone the chicken, chop it up and place it in a casserole dish with high sides and flat base. Add the other ingredients and the stock (calculate 700 ml of stock). Add the rice and the blood sausages cut into slices, spread them around the casserole dish and rectify with salt.
5. Bake at 250° C for 15 minutes. After this time, remove the casserole dish from the oven, Add the eggs well beaten with a pinch of salt so that they are well spread over the surface of the rice. Pierce the surface in several places with a knife so that the egg penetrates into the rice a little. Bake for 5 more minutes, turn off the oven and leave to rest 5 more minutes before serving.

The egg should be like a soufflé with a pretty golden colour, so be careful it does not burn.
If you want, you can sprinkle the surface of the rice with breadcrumbs after adding the beaten eggs.

valencian_cuisine

arròs a banda d'alacant
rice with seafood of alicante

for 4 people

* 400 g of rice * 1 kg of small fish for stock * 200 g of small peeled prawns * 250 g of small cuttlefish (*sepionets*) * 2 tomatoes * ½ red pepper * 2 ñoras * 2 cloves of garlic * saffron * olive oil * salt

1. Heat three spoonfuls of oil in a pan and fry the ñoras. Remove them and chop them. Add the whole cloves of garlic and the peppers cut in strips. Add the grated tomatoes, Season with a pinch of salt and leave to cook for 4 minutes.
2. Clean all the fish for the stock and place it in a pot. Cover with 2.5 l of water and add the sauce base from the pan (put the strips of pepper apart), the chopped ñoras, the saffron and salt. Bring to the boil and leave to cook on a low flame for 30 minutes.
3. Sauté the prawns in a paella dish with three spoonfuls of oil, remove them and put to one side. Add the cuttlefish, clean and chopped and cook them 3 more minutes. Add the rice and fry it all lightly for 2 more minutes.
4. Add the strips of pepper and pour in the strained stock (calculate double and a little more of stock than rice). Cook 8 minutes on a high flame, lower the intensity of the flame and leave to cook on a medium-low flame for 10 more minutes. A few minutes before ending the cooking add the prawns again.
5. Serve the rice with seafood accompanied with *allioli* sauce.

It can also be served with a typical *salmorreta* sauce made with soaked roast tomato with garlic, onion, parsley, chilli, vinegar, oil and salt.

arròs del senyoret
rice *del senyoret*

for 4 people

* 300 g of rice * 250 g of monkfish * 50 g of calamari slices * 50 g of baby squid
* 50 g of peeled prawns * 800 g of small fish or fish for stock * 2 cloves of garlic * 2 tomatoes
* saffron * olive oil * salt

1. Clean the small fish and place it in a casserole dish covered with 2.5 l of water. Bring to the boil, salt and leave to reduce for 25 minutes. Leave to rest and strain.
2. Clean the monkfish, baby squid, calamari and the prawns and cut everything into small pieces.
3. Make a cross cut in the base of the tomatoes and scald them for 2 minutes in a casserole dish with boiling water. Drain them, cool them under the cold tap, peel them, remove the pips and chop them.
4. Heat three spoonfuls of oil in a paella dish and fry the fish lightly in rounds. First the monkfish, then the calamari and baby squid and finally the prawns.
5. Add the chopped garlics, sauté for 1 minute and add the chopped tomato. Season and sauté for 2 more minutes.
6. Add the rice and the saffron, stir for a few moments and pour in the hot fish stock. Cook for 10 minutes on a high flame, lower the intensity and cook for eight more minutes on a medium-low flame. Leave to rest a few minutes before serving.

The name of this rice dish (little master) comes from fanciful way of preparing all the seafood, which must be clean and chopped.
The stock can be made with the heads and bones of the fish, as well as with the heads and shells of the prawns.

valencian_cuisine

paella valenciana

for 4 people

* 400 g of rice * 350 g of chicken * 350 g of rabbit * 2 tomatoes * 200 g of flat green beans (*bajoqueta* or *ferraura*) * 125 g of *garrofó* type young green beans * 125 g of *tavella* type tender kidney beans * saffron * 1 dl of olive oil * salt

1. Heat the oil in the paella dish and brown the meats. Remove the meats to the edges of the paella dish and add the flat green beans and peeled and chopped tomato in the centre. Fry all together lightly for a few minutes and add a litre of water. Add the kidney beans, the saffron and the salt.
2. Cook on a high flame, bring to the boil, lower the intensity of the flame and cook for 30 minutes. Replace the water that has been reduced, bring to the boil again and pour in the rice.
3. Cook for 10 minutes on a high flame and reduce the intensity of the flame. Cook for 8 more minutes on a medium-low flame. Leave to rest for 5 minutes before serving.

This is the paella recipe just as it is prepared in the Valencian orchards. In season you can add snails (*vaquetes*) or artichokes cut into quarters.

You can aromatise the stock with a small bunch of fresh rosemary that is later removed.

Although the saffron is a basic ingredient of the recipe, the intense yellow colour of some paellas is due to the use of food colouring.

You can season the sauce base with a little paprika.

valencian_cuisine

paella alicantina

para 4 personas

* 400 g of rice * 600 g of rabbit * 400 g of chicken * 250 g of lean pork * 1 red pepper
* 2 tomatoes * 150 g of cooked chick peas * 1 ñora * 2 cloves of garlic * stock of chicken
* saffron * 1 lemon * olive oil * salt

1. Chop up the chicken and the rabbit. Wash the pepper, remove the stem and the inner seeds and cut it into strips. Grate the tomatoes. Peel and chop the cloves of garlic.

2. Fry lightly the ñora with the strips of pepper in a paella dish with four spoonfuls of oil, remove them and put them aside. In the same oil brown all the meats and put them aside. Add the grated tomato and the two whole cloves of garlic. Cook until the tomato begins to change colour.

3. Remove the garlics and crush them in a mortar along with the ñora.

4. Add the rice to the paella, sauté for a few moments and pour in the hot stock (calculate double the stock to the rice). Add all the meats again, the strips of pepper, the chick peas and the crushed mix. Season with salt and some threads of saffron.

5. Cook on a high flame for 5 minutes. Lower the intensity of the flame and cook 12 more minutes. Decorate the paella with the strips of red pepper and segments of lemon. Leave to rest a few minutes before serving.

The stock can be prepared boiling the carcass of chicken along with the rabbit bones, leek, carrot, celery, a tomato, a ñora, salt and some threads of saffron.

paella de castelló
paella castellonense

for 4 people

* 400 g of rice * 200 g of chicken * 200 g of rabbit * 100 g of pork rib * 100 g of green beans
* 1 red pepper * 1 ripe tomato * 1 small bunch of parsley * 2 cloves of garlic * olive oil * saffron
* salt

1. Chop the chicken, the rabbit and the rib. Wash the pepper, dry it and cut it into strips. Peel and chop the tomato. Peel and chop the garlics. Wash the beans, trim them and cut them into pieces of 4 cm. Chop the parsley finely. Bring water or stock to the boil in a casserole dish apart.
2. Heat four spoonfuls of oil in the paella dish and sauté all the meats until they are browned. Remove them and put them aside.
3. In the same oil lightly fry the pepper, the tomato, the parsley and the garlics. Add the green beans and sauté all together for a few moments.
4. Place the meats in the paella dish again and pour in the hot water or stock (calculate double the stock to that of rice). Season with salt and saffron, stir for a few seconds and leave to cook 18 minutes. Leave to rest for 5 minutes before serving.

A different type of paella is the one prepared in Valencia's Ribera Alta. It includes green peppers, ferraura, tavella and garrofó, tomato, garlic, saffron, rabbit and snails. In people's homes they usually also add meatballs made with pork, hen's liver and blood and aromatised with garlic, parsley, pine nuts and cinnamon..

valencian_cuisine

paella de marisc
seafood paella

for 4 people

* 400 g of rice * 500 g of small fish for stock * 500 g of mussels * 250 g of monkfish * 1 cuttlefish * 4 prawns * 4 Dublin bay prawns * 2 tomatoes * 3 cloves of garlic * olive oil * saffron * salt

1. Prepare a fish stock boiling a lot of water with the small fish, the monkfish bone if available, a clove of garlic, some threads of saffron and a pinch of salt. Bring to the boil and leave to reduce by half.
2. Open the mussels by steaming and remove empty half shells. Strain part of the cooking juice and add it to the stock.
3. Clean the cuttlefish removing the cuttlebone, guts, eyes and beak. Cut it into cubes. Cut the monkfish into cubes. Grate the tomato. Peel and crush the garlics.
4. Heat four spoonfuls of oil in a paella dish and sauté the prawns and the Dublin bay prawns briefly. Remove them, season them with a pinch of salt and put them aside.
5. In the same oil, sauté the cubes of cuttlefish and monkfish for 4 minutes. Remove them, salt them and put them aside.
6. Add the grated tomato and two crushed garlics and cook for 5 minutes. Add the cubes of cuttlefish again and add the rice. Sauté a few moments and cover with the hot strained stock (calculate double the stock to the rice).
7. Rectify with salt if necessary and add some threads of saffron. Cook for 5 minutes on a high flame.
8. After this time, place the mussels, Dublin bay prawns and prawns decoratively. Cook for 12 more minutes on a medium-low flame and leave to rest a few minutes before serving.

The variations of the seafood or marine paella, typical in a restaurant, are infinite. They can be combined with other sea ingredients such as calamari, clams, spottail mantis squillid, crabs, king prawns…

valencian_cuisine

paella de bacallà i col-i-flor
cod and cauliflower paella

for 4 people

* 400 g of rice * 200 g of desalted cod * ¼ of cauliflower * 2 cloves of garlic * 1 tomato
* ½ teaspoon of paprika * saffron * olive oil * salt

1. Dry the cod well and grill it lightly on a hot paella pan. Then crumble it up with your fingers.
2. Wash the cauliflower and cut it into branches. Peel and chop the cloves of garlic.
3. Heat three spoonfuls of oil in a paella dish and lightly fry the tomato with the chopped garlics. When the tomato begins to change colour, add the crumbled cod and the branches of cauliflower.
4. Season with the paprika, salt and some threads of saffron and cover with water (calculate the double the water than rice). Cook for 5 minutes on a high flame and then cook another 12 minutes on a medium-low flame. Leave to rest a few minutes before serving.

This Lent rice dish can also be prepared in the oven. There are many rice dishes with cod that include other ingredients such as spinach, young garlics, onion, pork chops…
Bandit's rice (arròs ofls roders) is made with the ingredients that fugitives could take to their hideouts in the mountain: cod, garlic, saffron, dried peppers, snails and wild herbs.

valencian_cuisine

160_orange and cod salad
162_salted tuna, tomato, orange and black olive salad
165_*esgarraet*
166_*espencat*
168_*mullador of sangatxo*
171_*pericana* sauce
172_stew of the plain
174_octopus stew
177_noodles
178_flat breads of *mullador*
180_flat bread a *la calfor*
183_frigate mackerel stew with spinach
184_*giraboix*
186_shrimps with swiss chard
189_musician's stew
190_stuffed peppers
192_stew

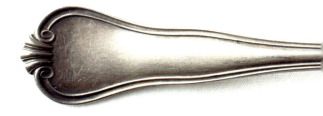

recipes of starters

valencian_cuisine

amanida de taronja i bacallà
orange and cod salad

for 4 people

* 3 oranges * 2 spring onions * 300 g of desalted cod * 2 spoonfuls of black olives
<u>for the vinaigrette</u>:
* 4 spoonfuls of olive oil * 1 spoonful of Jerez vinegar * pepper * salt

1. Peel the spring onions, cut them into thin segments and leave them in a bowl with water and ice for 15 minutes so they lose their intensity.

2. Drain the cod and cut it into strips. Peel the oranges to the flesh, removing all the white skin, and cut them into segments.

3. Prepare the vinaigrette mixing the oil with the vinegar and a pinch of salt and pepper until obtaining an emulsified sauce.

4. Place the orange segments decoratively forming a fan on a dish and place the cod in the centre. Sprinkle over the spring onions and black olives, season with the vinaigrette and serve.

In the Valencia Community the cod known commonly as "English" or green cod is very popular, half cured, less salted than the Norwegian or Icelandic white cods.

valencian_cuisine

amanida de moixama, tomàquet, taronja i olives negres
salted tuna, tomato, orange and black olive salad

for 4 people

* 4 salad tomatoes * 150 g of salted tuna * 1 orange * 2 spoonfuls of pine nuts * 2 spoonfuls of black olives * 3 spoonfuls of olive oil * 1 spoonful of vinegar * 1 spoonful of sugar * 1 small bunch of parsley * pepper * salt

1. Wash the orange under the tap, dry it and finely grate the peel. Squeeze it to obtain the juice.
2. Heat the orange juice in a small saucepan with the sugar until obtaining a syrup. Add the vinegar, cook for a few minutes more and leave to cool.
3. Peel the tomatoes and cut them into small cubes. Place them in a bowl with the grated orange peel and the chopped parsley. Season with a pinch of salt and dress with the oil. Leave to macerate for 10 minutes.
4. Meanwhile, toast the pine nuts in a non-stick pan with a drop of oil until they begin to take colour. Cut the salted cod in very thin slices.
5. De-stone the olives and crush them with a little oil until attaining a thick purée.
6. Using a metal ring assemble the salads on the plates. First place a layer of the tomato cubes, then some slices of salted tuna and end with a layer of tomato. Sprinkle the chopped pine nuts and pour on the orange syrup and some drops of black olive purée. Serve immediately.

Salted tuna is often served as an appetiser, with some good extra virgin olive oil on top and accompanied with tomato or with toasted almonds.

esgarraet

for 4 people

* 3 pimientos rojos * 2 lomitos de bacalao inglés * 2 dientes de ajo * aceite de oliva

1. Lightly spread the peppers with a thread of olive oil and roast them in the pre-heated oven at 200° C for 50 minutes. Wrap them in silver foil and leave them to cool. Then peel them, remove the stem and the inner seeds and cut them into strips.
2. Place the strips of roast pepper in a salad bowl with the garlic cut into fine slices and the fillets of cod crumbled up. Stir, cover with olive oil and with kitchen paper. Leave to rest in the fridge for a few hours.
3. Serve the *esgarraet* accompanied with toasted bread.

If possible, it is a good idea to roast the peppers on the grill. They then acquire a delicious note smoky flavour.
The English cod is less salty. If you use a different type of cod for this dish desalt it slightly leaving it to soak.

valencian_cuisine

espencat
espencat

for 4 people

* 2 aubergines * 1 red pepper * 1 green pepper * 1 onion * 1 garlic * olive oil

1. Place the aubergines, peppers and onion on an oven tray and roast them in a preheated oven at 200º C for 50 minutes. Then remove the pepper and wrap them in tin foil. Continue cooking the aubergine and onion for another 20 minutes.

2. Wrap the aubergine and onion in tin foil. Leave all the roast vegetables to cool and then peel and them into strips.

3. Place the strips of roast vegetables on a tray and add the very finely chopped garlic. Pour lots of extra virgin olive oil over and leave in the fridge for a few hours before serving.

This dish is often confused with esgarraet. It has many local variants. In some places it is made without the green pepper and onion and in other cases, however, they add roast tomato.
It can be served with anchovies, strips of poor cod, cod, tuna steak or thin slices of dried octopus.
Chopped hard-boiled egg or capers are also often added.

valencian_cuisine

mullador de sangatxo
mullador of sangatxo

for 4 people

* 400 g of *sangatxo* * 4 tomatoes * 1 aubergine * 2 red peppers * 1 green pepper * 2 potatoes
* 1 teaspoon of paprika * 2 cloves of garlic * a fistful of almonds * 1 slice of bread * olive oil * salt

1. Leave to soak the *sangatxo* for 4 or 5 hours in warm water, changing it several times so that it is well desalted. Drain it and dry it with kitchen paper.

2. Make a cross cut in the base of the tomatoes, scald them for 2 minutes in a casserole dish with boiling water. Peel them and chop them. Peel the potatoes and cut them into pieces od 2 cm. wash the peppers, dry them and cut them into squares of the same size. Wash the aubergine and cut it into squares the same size as the peppers.

3. Heat four spoonfuls of oil in a casserole dish and lightly sauté the *sangatxo*. Drain it and put it to one side.

4. In the same oil lightly fry the peeled garlics, the almonds and the chopped bread. When they start to take on colour, remove them and crush them in the mortar or the bowl of the mixer.

5. In the same oil, sauté the peppers and the aubergine for 10 minutes. Add the chopped tomato and sauté 5 more minutes. Season with paprika and cover with boiling water. Add the potatoes and the paste and bring to the boil. Lower the intensity of the flame and cook on a low flame for 30 minutes, stirring frequently.

6. When there are 10 minutes left for the cooking, add the *sangatxo* again. Before serving, rectify with a pinch of salt.

Sangatxo is obtained from a part of the tuna, stuck to the bones, where the coagulated blood of the fish is deposited. Just like the *bull* it is used in numerous stews and recipes of a popular nature. This recipe, typical of Marina Alta in Alicante, also has the name of *tomacat* or "fritanga".

pericana
pericana

for 4 people

∗ 4 dried red peppers ∗ 100 g of dried poor cod or cod ∗ 3 cloves of garlic ∗ virgin extra olive oil

1. Sauté the dry peppers in a pan with very hot oil until they begin to brown. Leave them to cool and break them into pieces.
2. Grill the garlic in a pan or in the oven and cut them into laminas. Also sauté the cod or the poor cod (or grill them over charcoal) and cut them up.
3. Mix all the prepared ingredients on a dish. Add the oil with which you have sautéed the peppers and leave to one side for at least 30 minutes so that the peppers are rehydrated.
4. Serve the pericana as an appetizer with some toasties.

The dry peppers can be baked in the oven. You can add ñoras, dried tomatoes and a pinch of paprika. Other variants of this recipe are the "fresh *pericana*" (with strips of roast pepper) and the "*pericana* in salad", with tomato and chopped spring onions. In Elche this dish is known as pipes i carasses.

valencian_cuisine

olla de la plana
stew of la plana

for 6 people

* 250 g of kidney beans * 100 g of green beans * 250 g of cabbage * 2 cardoon leaves
* 4 Swiss chard leaves * 1 carrot * 1 turnip * 2 potatoes * 1 onion * 2 tomatoes
* 2 cups of rice (optional) * 3 garlics * saffron * paprika * olive oil * salt

1. Leave the kidney beans to soak overnight. The next day, place them in a large casserole dish, cover with a lot of water and bring to the boil. Stop the boiling three times adding cold water and removing the foam that forms on the surface.

2. Cook the kidney beans for an hour and a half or until they are tender.

3. Add all the vegetables, washed, peeled and cut into cubes, into the pot. Cook on a low flame for another 15 minutes. Season with a little salt and some threads of saffron. Add the rice, if you want, and cook for 15 more minutes.

4. Sauté the chopped onion in a pan with three spoonfuls of oil until it begins to brown. Add the chopped garlic, grated tomatoes and paprika, stir and remove from the flame.

5. Add this sauce base to the pot and cook all together for another 5 minutes. Leave to one side a few minutes and serve.

This popular stew from Castellón can also be made with chickpeas and other fresh vegetables, such as pumpkin or parsnips.

valencian_cuisine

putxero de polp
octopus stew

for 6 people

* 1.5 kg of cleaned octopus * 250 g of kidney beans or chick peas soaked the night before * 150 g of fresh white bacon * 2 *blanquets* * 1 celery * 1 leek * 1 turnip * 1 parsnip * 2 carrots * 4 very tender green leaves * ¼ cabbage * 4 potatoes * 1 tomato * 1 onion * 1 teaspoon of paprika * a fistful of chopped almonds * 1 whole garlic * saffron * 300 g of rice * olive oil * salt
<u>for the filling</u>:

* 200 g of minced pork * 200 g of minced beef * 1 chicken liver * 1 spoonful of pine nuts * 1 egg * 2 spoonfuls of breadcrumbs * 1 teaspoon of paprika * grated lemon peel

1. Prepare the filling mixing all the ingredients and fill the octopus heads. Sew them so that they do not break open.
2. Heat three spoonfuls of oil in an iron pot and sauté the octopus, the peeled and chopped tomato, the almonds and the whole garlic. Sauté all together for a few minutes.
3. When the octopus begins to take on colour, add the kidney beans and pour in 6 litres of cold water (hot if you use chick peas). Add the bacon, the *blanquets* and the rest of the vegetables, peeled and chopped (except the potato). Season with salt, pepper, paprika and saffron and cook on a medium flame for 2 hours or until the beans are tender. Add the potatoes half way through cooking.
4. Separate the stock and use it to prepare soupy or syrupy rice dish. Serve the soupy rice as a starter and then the octopus with the pulses and other vegetables, all presented decoratively on a large platter.

This lavish dish of the fishermen of Calpe has become a sign of identity of the gastronomy of Benissa and Moraira.
In season sweet potato can be added.

fideuà
noodles

for 6 people

* 500 g of number 3 noodles * 6 prawns * 6 Dublin bay prawns * 1 medium size cuttlefish
* 150 g of natural tomato * 1.5 kg of small fish or stock fish * 1 spoonful of paprika
* 1 branch of parsley * 1 clove of garlic * saffron * olive oil * salt

1. Cover the small fish with a lot of water, add salt and leave to reduce for 40 minutes until obtaining one and a half litres of fish stock. Cover and put to one side.
2. Prepare a mix in the mortar with the garlic clove, parsley and a few threads of saffron.
3. Heat some spoonfuls of oil in a paella pan and brown the Dublin bay prawns and prawns. Remove them and put to one side.
4. In the same oil, sauté the cleaned and chopped cuttlefish. Add the paprika, stir and add the tomato and sauce mix from the mortar. Cook for a few minutes and pour the hot stock and add a pinch of salt if necessary.
5. Bring to the boil, lower the intensity of the flame and cook slowly for another 10 minutes. After just two minutes cooking place the Dublin bay prawns and prawns decoratively over the noodles.
6. Remove the pan from the flame and leave to rest for a few minutes so that the noodles end up absorbing all the stock before serving.

You can add 400 g of monkfish cut into cubes and a chopped calamari. They say that this recipe was invented by some fishermen in the high seas when they realised they had forgotten the rice for the pot.

valencian_cuisine

coques de mullador
flat breads of *mullador*

for 9 small flat breads

<u>for the dough:</u> * 500 g of flour * 25 g of baker's yeast * 2 dl (1 cup) of warm water
* 1 dl (½ cup) of olive oil

<u>for the topping:</u> * ½ kg of tomatoes * 2 onions * 2 green peppers * 2 red peppers
* 2 aubergines * 18 anchovies * 1 teaspoonful of sweet paprika * olive oil * salt

1. For the dough: mix the flour in an earthenware bowl with the crumbled yeast, oil, warm water and salt. Knead with your fists until obtaining a uniform dough. Break up the dough and knead again. Repeat this operation until the dough no longer sticks to the side of the bowl. Shape nine balls the size of a lemon, cover them with a cloth and leave them to rest for 15-20 minutes.

2. For the *mullador* of onion and tomato: clean half of the tomatoes, peel them and cut them up finely. Peel and chop the onions. Sauté both ingredients in a casserole dish with some spoonfuls of olive oil. Season with a pinch of paprika and salt. leave this sauce base to drain in a sieve so that all the liquid filters through.

3. For the *mullador* of pepper and tomato: clean, peel and cut the rest of the tomatoes. Clean and chop the green peppers. Leave to drain raw in a sieve.

4. For the *mullador* of red peppers and aubergine: roast the vegetables in a preheated oven at 200° C: the peppers for 50 minutes and the aubergines for 1 hour 10 minutes. Wrap in tin foil, leave to cool, peel and cut into strips.

5. Place three balls of dough on a lightly oiled baking tray and flatten them with your fingertips until obtaining three small flat breads. Spread a few spoonfuls of the fillings over each one and place two anchovies on top. Bake the flat breads at 200° C for 20 minutes. Repeat the operation with the other ingredients until obtaining nine flat breads.

Other typical ingredients for the mullador are salted tuna, frigate mackerel, onions and peas, Swiss chard or spinach with garlic…

valencian_cuisine

coques a la calfor
flat bread a la *calfor*

for 15 flat breads

for the dough:

* 2 cups of wheat flour * 1 cup of corn flour * 3.5 cups of water * 1 onion * a dash of olive oil * a pinch of salt

for the fillings:

* spinach or Swiss chard cooked and reheated with garlics, small prawns and cod * fried tomato, tuna, anchovies and roast peppers

1. Finely grate the onion and put it in a casserole dish with the amount of water indicated, a dash of oil and a pinch of salt. Bring to the boil and cook for a few minutes, until the onion is cooked.
2. Add all together the two types of flour and mix with force using a spatula for removing all the lumps that form.
3. Heat water in a bigger casserole dish, remove from the flame and place the smaller one with the dough in it as if it were a bain-marie so that the dough is hot while we work on it.
4. Remove the dough from the pot when it is a ball that does not stick to the side of the pot, place it on a plate with a dash of oil and make small dough balls in line.
5. Squash the small balls with a flat object to obtain small pancakes and put them aside in a recipient between sheets of kitchen or baking paper.
6. Heat a drop of oil or lard in a pan and fry the flat breads on both sides. Serve them immediately accompanied with the fillings indicated.

These flat breads are typical of the county of La Safor. Many families from the areas of Gandía, Oliva, Rotova and Bellreguard use heavy circular-shaped wooden moulds, made especially by the local carpenters to give shape to the flat breads more easily.

borreta de melva amb espinacs
frigate mackerel stew with spinach

for 4 people

* 300 g of salted frigate mackerel * 150 g of spinach * 2 dried tomatoes * 1 onion * 2 potatoes
* 1 whole garlic * 1 soupspoon of flour * 1 teaspoon of paprika * 1 small bunch of parsley
* olive oil * salt

1. Leave the frigate mackerel to soak for 4 hours changing the water several times. Then boil it for 10 minutes and cool it with water and ice. Drain and chop it.

2. Sauté the whole garlic on a low flame in a casserole dish with three spoonfuls of oil. Add the potatoes cut into slices and the dried tomatoes, previously rehydrated in water. Sauté for a few minutes, cover with water and add the spinach and the chopped parsley.

3. Dilute the flour in half a cup of water and pour it over the stew. Add the chopped frigate mackerel and the paprika. Cook together on a low flame for about 10 minutes. Rectify with salt if necessary and serve.

There are many local variants of this dish, very popular in the south of Valencia and in the Alicante counties. You can use ñoras instead of paprika and add cod, cuttlefish, chopped tomato, onion, artichokes or other vegetables.
It is very typical to break an egg so that it cooks in the stock in the final minutes.

valencian_cuisine

giraboix

for 4 people

* 200 g of cod * 1 onion * 4 potatoes * 150 g of green beans * 350 g of Swiss chard leaves * 1 *blanquet* * 1 black pudding * 4 slices of brown bread * 2 dl of olive oil * 1 egg yolk * 1 garlic clove * 4 hard-boiled eggs * 1 ripe tomato * 1 ñora * salt

1. Leave the cod to soak for the time necessary according to its thickness, changing the water several times.
2. Prepare the *allioli* in the traditional way with a mortar and egg yolk, pouring in a thread of oil and using an electric mixer.
3. Boil the Swiss chard leaves with the beans, the onion, the cod, the black pudding, the *blanquet* and the tomato. Bring to the boil and, after 10 minutes, add the potatoes peeled and cut into large pieces. Cook on a medium flame for 20 more minutes.
4. Drain the stock and remove the black pudding, the *blanquet*, the ñora and the tomato. Cut all into small pieces and place it in a casserole dish apart. Add the hard-boiled eggs cut into very thin slices and mix. Add the slices of brown bread, toasted and crumbled. Season with spoonfuls of *allioli* to taste and pour in the hot stock.
5. Serve the soup on one side and the cod with the potatoes, Swiss chard, beans and onion in another bowl, lightly covered with a little *allioli*.

This recipe is typical of the villages of the mountainous areas of Alicante, such as Ibi, Tibi or Xixona. A popular refrain goes *"Si the reina sabés que és giraboix, vindria de Madrid a llepar the boix"* ("If the queen knew about *giraboix*, she would come from Madrid to lick the mortar").
The soup can also be served with the *allioli* apart so that each person dresses it to taste. Variants are also made with cabbage, skate and small prawns or with chicken and rabbit.

valencian_cuisine

gamba amb bleda
shrimps with swiss chard

for 8 people (as an appetiser)

* 300 g of Swiss chard * 200 g of marshland prawns or shrimps * 2 cloves of garlic * 1 teaspoon of paprika * ½ cup of white wine * olive oil * salt

1. Wash the Swiss chard under the tap, drain and chop it. Cook it in a casserole dish with boiling salted water for 20 minutes. Drain it and keep it in a cup of the cooking water.

2. Heat three spoonfuls of oil in a pan with the chopped garlic without letting it change colour. Add the shrimps and cook for one minute. Then sprinkle with the paprika and add the Swiss chard and a cup of the cooking water.

3. Cook all together on a low flame for a few minutes until all the water has been absorbed. Rectify with salt if necessary and serve immediately as an appetiser, starter or filling for the flat breads *a la calfor*.

Despite the name, this typical appetiser from the county of La Safor is not prepared with prawns but the small river shrimps traditionally from the marshland of Pego-Oliva.

olleta de músics
musician's stew

for 6 people

* 250 g of kidney beans * 1 turnip * 250 g of cardoon leaves * 50 g of pig offal (*freixura*) * 50 g of bacon * 50 g of pig's heart (*coraeta*) * 50 g of lean pork meat * 50 g of pork ribs * 2 onion black puddings * 1 onion * 2 litres of water * some threads of saffron * a pinch of paprika * some thyme leaves * olive oil * fresh ground black pepper * salt

1. Leave the kidney beans to soak overnight covered with water. Clean the cardoon leaves and boil them in water to blanch them and take away the bitterness. As soon as the water boils drain them and put aside.
2. Sauté the chopped onion in a pan with two spoonfuls of oil until it is transparent. Add a pinch of paprika and put aside.
3. Bring the kidney beans to the boil in a casserole dish with a lot of water. As soon as it boils, remove the water and add the leaves and the reheated onion. Cover again with two litres of water and add the chopped turnip and all the meats. Season with salt, pepper, saffron and a few leaves of thyme and cover.
4. Leave to cook on a low flame for 2 hours, adding some cold water several times for the cooking.

In some villages rice is added to the stew. In Alcoy they say the authentic *olleta de músics* does not contain it, since it was a dish they gave to the musicians in the festivals of Moors and Christians and thus avoided the rice from overcooking when they ate it after playing.
The black puddings must be in pieces. If you want them to be more whole you should add them in the final minutes.

valencian_cuisine

pebreres farcides
stuffed peppers

for 4 people

- 8 medium red peppers * 400 g of rice * 300 g of fine green beans (*fesols de careta*)
- 125 g of slated tuna (*tonyina of tronc*) * 2 ripe tomatoes * 1 small bunch of parsley
- ½ litre of stock * 2 spoonfuls of pine nuts * 3 cloves of garlic * ½ teaspoon of cinnamon
- some threads of saffron * 125 ml of olive oil * salt

1. The evening before cut the tuna into cubes and leave them to soak covered with water. Change the water several times.
2. Wash the peppers, dry and cut the upper part as if it were a tapa. Remove the seeds and salt the inside. Remove the stems of the tapas and cut them into pieces.
3. Peel and chop the cloves of garlic. Grate a tomato and cut the other into eight slices. Wash and chop the parsley finely.
4. Heat the oil in a wide casserole dish and sauté the pieces of pepper with the chopped garlics until they begin to soften. Add the grated tomato, stir and add the tuna. Sprinkle with parsley and add the pine nuts. Season with a pinch of cinnamon, add the chopped green beans and leave to cook on a very low flame for about 10 minutes.
5. Add the saffron and cover with half a litre of stock. Bring to the boil and cook for about 8 minutes. Add the rice and cook for 2 more minutes (the rice should be almost raw).
6. Stuff the peppers with the preparation and cover them with a slice of tomato seasoned with salt. Cover the bowl with very wet baking paper and bake at 250° C for 1½ hours. Lower the temperature to 170° C and cook them for 30 more minutes.

You should choose medium-size red peppers that are straight in order to stuff them easily. This recipe is typical of Oliva, in the county of La Safor but there are many variants. They are also called *bajoques farcides*.

valencian_cuisine

putxero
stew

for 8 people

* 400 g of beef shank * 250 g of hen * 150 g of pig's trotter * 100 g of fresh bacon * 1 marrowbone * 1 ham bone * 2 *blanquets* * 2 chorizos * 2 onion black puddings * 100 g of pork rib * 250 g of soaked chick peas * 2 potatoes * 1 sweet potato * 150 g of cardoon leaves * 1 turnip * 1 carrot * 1 parsnip * 1 leek * 1 stick of celery * some threads of saffron * 150 g of noodles for the soup * salt

<u>for the *pilotes*:</u>

* 250 g of minced pork * 250 g of minced beef * 2 eggs * 100 g of chicken liver * 1 small bunch of parsley * 4 slices of bread soaked in milk * A pinch of cinnamon, nutmeg and pepper * 1 grated lemon peel * 50 g of lard * egg white for coating * salt

1. Prepare the *pilotes* massing all the well chopped ingredients. With moist hands, form thick oval-shaped meatballs. Coat them in egg white.

2. In a large high-sided pot add the meats and the chick peas in a mesh bag. Cover generously with water, season with salt and saffron and bring to the boil. Remove the froth from the stock several times and leave to cook on a low flame. After an hour, add all the cleaned and chopped vegetables. Cook for another 1½ hours. When there are 20 minutes to go, add the *pilotes*.

3. Strain part of the stock and boil it with fine noodles to prepare the soup. Serve the soup first, followed by a bowl with the cooked meatballs and finally, the meats, chick peas and vegetables.

You can make savoury and sweet meatballs. Season the latter with sugar, cinnamon, nutmeg and grated lemon peel.

valencian_cuisine

03

196_*all i pebre* of eels
198_*blanquillo* of monkfish
201_sea bass stew
202_*cruet* of eel and vegetables
204_*llandeta* of red mullet
207_octopus with cardoon leaves
208_*figatells*
210_gazpacho of rabbit and chicken
213_*tombet* of lamb with snails

main course recipes

valencian_cuisine

all i pebre d'anguiles
all i pebre of eels

for 4 people

* 1 kg of chopped eels * 5 medium size potatoes * 1 chilli * 1 whole garlic * 1 spoonful of paprika * 100 ml of oil * 1 laurel leaf * 2 slices of bread * a fistful of almonds or pine nuts * 1 small bunch of parsley * pepper * salt

1. Peel and chop the potatoes. Crush the garlics lightly without peeling them.
2. Heat the oil in a casserole dish and lightly fry the slices of bread until they brown. Remove them and put them aside. Add the garlic and remove the casserole dish from the flame. Let the garlics reheat a few moments in the hot oil without browning and put the casserole dish back on the stove.
3. Add the paprika and the laurel leaf, wet with a cup of water and add the potatoes and chopped eels. Cover with water, season and add the chilli. Leave to cook on a high flame for about 25 minutes, adding a little more water if necessary.
4. Prepare a sauce base in the mortar grinding the almonds with the fried bread, a couple of garlic cloves and a little parsley. Add this base to the *all i pebre* half way through cooking. Serve hot.

The potatoes must be cut in wedges or broken so that more starch is released and the stock thickens. If you want, you can add a pinch of cinnamon. The variant with chicken is known as *espardenyà*.
This recipe, typical of the lagoon area, can also be used with all kinds of fish.

valencian_cuisine

blanquillo de rap
blanquillo of monkfish

for 4 people

* 650 g of monkfish * 2 potatoes * 1 turnip * 150 g of cardoon leaves * 150 g of flat green beans * 1 carrot * 1 laurel leaf * 1 small bunch of parsley * 2 cloves of garlic * 2 ñoras * 1 large tomato * olive oil * salt

for the *allioli*:

* 2 dl of olive oil * 1 egg * 1 garlic clove * 1 spoonful of lemon juice * a pinch of salt

1. Peel the potatoes and the carrots. Wash the cardoon leaves and the green beans. Chop all the vegetables. Wash the parsley, dry it and chop it finely. Clean the monkfish, cut it into small pieces or slices and season it.

2. Prepare an allioli mixing all the ingredients in the bowl of the blender until obtaining a uniform sauce. (You can also make it in the traditional way crushing the garlic in the mortar with a pinch of salt and gradually add the oil in a thread).

3. Heat three spoonfuls of oil in a casserole dish and brown the ñoras. Add the slightly crushed remaining garlics. Remove the ñoras, crush them in a mortar and add them again. Add the tomato, peeled and chopped, and the parsley and sauté for a few minutes.

4. Add all the vegetables to the casserole dish, sauté a few moments and cover with a litre of water or fish stock. Add a laurel leaf, season and bring to the boil. Lower the intensity of the flame and leave to cook for about 15 minutes.

5. Add the slices of monkfish and leave to cook together for 10 more minutes. Dilute two spoonfuls of the allioli in a cup of the stock and add to the casserole dish at the last moment. Serve immediately nice and hot.

This marine stew is typical of the coastal villages south of Alicante and the island of Tabarca.
It can be prepared with any type of fish.

caldereta de llobarro
sea bass stew

for 4 people

* 900 g of sea bass * 4 large prawns * 250 g of mussels * 200 g of clams * 2 tomatoes * 1 onion
* 2 potatoes * 1 red pepper * 3 cloves of garlic * 1 cbioled egg yolk * 1 teaspoon of paprika
* 1 litre of fish stock * 1 small bunch of parsley * olive oil * pepper * salt

1. Leave the clams to soak in a bowl of water with a lot of salt for a minimum of 6 hours so that all the sand they may contain is expelled. Clean the mussels and remove the side threads. Clean the sea bass, remove the scales and guts and cut it into pieces.
2. Wash the tomatoes, Peel and chop them. Peel and chop the onion and the cloves of garlic. Wash the pepper and cut it into squares. Peel the potatoes and cut them into slices. Wash the parsley and chop it finely.
3. Heat three spoonfuls of oil in a casserole dish and sauté the onion on a very low flame for 10 minutes. Add two chopped garlic cloves and the red pepper, cook 2 more minutes and add the chopped tomato. Season, sprinkle with the paprika and leave to cook on a very low flame for 5 more minutes.
4. Then add the potatoes and cover with the hot fish stock. Bring to the boil and cook for 10 minutes. Add the fish and cook 5 more minutes.
5. Prepare a sauce base in the mortar with the remaining chopped garlic, egg yolk and parsley. Add to the casserole dish and stir. Add the mussels, clams and prawns and cook together for 3-4 more minutes. Serve immediately.

This dish is often also prepared with roe or with other fish with a firm and tasty meat.

valencian_cuisine

cruet de congre i verdures
cruet of conger eel and vegetables

for 4 people

* 750 g of conger eel in slices or other fish * 2 potatoes * 1 tomato * 1 onion * 2 artichokes
* 100 g of peas * 100 g of broad beans * 1 small bunch of parsley * 1 carrot * 2 cloves of garlic
* 1 lemon * olive oil * pepper * salt

1. Peel the potatoes and cut them into fine slices. Peel the carrots and cut them into laminas. Peel the onion and cut it into slices. Shell the broad beans and peas. Clean the artichokes, cut them into quarters and rub them with the lemon juice so that they do not blacken. Peel and chop the tomato.
2. Heat three spoonfuls of oil in a casserole dish and add the sliced potatoes and onion, the artichokes in quarters, the chopped tomato, the carrots in laminas, the broad beans and the peas.
3. Add the conger eel, season and sprinkle with abundant chopped parsley. Cover slightly with water or stock and leave to cook for about 15 minutes until the vegetables have absorbed practically all the stock.
4. Prepare a mixture in the mortar with the cloves of garlic and parsley and add it to the casserole dish when there are 5 minutes left of the cooking. Serve immediately.

Cruet or *cru* means "raw", since all the ingredients of the recipe are added to the casserole dish raw. The same recipe can also be prepared in the oven calculating about 25 minutes at 180° C. As a typical fishermen's dish, the *cruet* has variations with an infinite number of fish of the most diverse quality and with other seasonal vegetables.

valencian_cuisine

llandeta de molls
llandeta of red mullet

for 4 people

* 800 g of red mullet * 3 potatoes * 2 tomatoes * 2 onions * 2 spoonfuls of pine nuts
* 3 cloves of garlic * 1 cup of water * 1 small bunch of parsley * 1 chilli * 1 teaspoon of paprika
* 6 spoonfuls of olive oil * salt

1. Peel the potatoes and cut them into slices. Peel the onion and cut it into fine slices. Peel the garlics and cut them into laminas. Clean the red mullets removing the scales and guts and season them.

2. Cover the base of a casserole dish or baking tray with the slices of potatoes. Season and add on top the onions, chilli, garlic laminas, tomato in slices and pine nuts. Season again and add the red mullet on top. Sprinkle with paprika and chopped parsley.

3. Pour in the water and oil and cook on a very low flame for 25 minutes, wetting the fish now and again with the stock so that they do not dry. Serve nice and hot.

To prepare this dish in larger quantities it is better to use the oven, firstly roasting the vegetables for about 20 minutes. Then add the fish and bake for 15 more minutes.
The *llandeta* can be prepared with other fish such as whiting, cuttlefish, conger eel, crabs, largehead hairtail…

polp amb penques
octopus with cardoon leaves

for 4 people

* 1 kg of cleaned octopus * 3 young cardoon leaves * 450 g of potatoes * 1 onion * 1 tomato * 8 almonds * 1 slice of bread * 2 cloves of garlic * 1 small bunch of parsley * 1 teaspoon of paprika * 1 dl of red wine * 1 laurel leaf * 1 lemon * olive oil * pepper * salt

1. Break up the bread and fry it with hot olive oil together with the almonds. Crush the bread, almonds, some leaves of parsley and a garlic clove in a mortar.
2. Cook the octopus in a casserole dish with abundant boiling salted water, a laurel leaf and the red wine for 40 minutes. Drain it, cut it up and put to one side. Also save the stock.
3. Clean the cardoon leaves, remove the threads and cut them up. Cook them in a casserole dish with boiling water and a few drops of lemon juice for 45 minutes. Drain them and refresh them with water and ice to stop the cooking.
4. Sauté the chopped onion in a casserole dish with three spoonfuls of oil until it is transparent. Add the remaining chopped garlic and the tomato, peeled and chopped. Season and cook for 5 more minutes.
5. Add the peeled and cut potatoes, octopus and cardoon leaves to the casserole dish. Season with the paprika, Cover with the octopus stock water and cook on a low flame for 30 minutes or until the potatoes are tender. 10 minutes before the end of cooking, add the mixture from the mortar. Serve nice and hot.

This recipe is typical of the marine cuisine of Alicante. To give a touch of sweetness to the stew you can add an ounce of chocolate. To ensure the octopus is tender you should freeze it and then defreeze it. This breaks the fibres of the meat.

valencian_cuisine

figatells
figatells

for 4 people

* 250 g of pig's liver * 250 g of lean pork meat * 1 small bunch of parsley * pork tripe membrane * 2 spoonfuls of pine nuts * 1 small bunch of parsley * ½ teaspoon of cloves * ¼ of teaspoon of cinnamon * ¼ of teaspoon of nutmeg * freshly ground black pepper * salt

1. Mince the two meats well. Wash the parsley, dry it and chop it finely. Mix the meats in a large bowl and add the chopped parsley. Season it with salt, pepper, clove, cinnamon and nutmeg. Stir well until it is all well mixed.

2. With moist hands, form slightly flattened meatballs. Extend the tripe membrane over a work surface and place the meatballs on top, separated from each other. Cut the membrane and wrap the meatballs.

3. Then flatten them to turn them into small hamburgers. Grill them with some drops of oil on a grill and serve immediately.

This recipe is very popular in the counties of El Safor, Ribera Baja, Marina Alta and l'Alcoià.

valencian_cuisine

gazpacho of rabbit and chicken

gaspatxo de conill i pollastre

for 4 people

* 300 g of chopped rabbit * 300 g of chopped chicken * 2 tomatoes * 1 onion * 1 bunch of *pebrella* (*Thymus piperella*) or thyme * 1 laurel leaf * 250 g of gazpacho bread * 2 cloves of garlic * olive oil * pepper * salt

1. Season the meats and cook the in a pot with abundant salted water. Cook until they are tender.
2. In the *gazpachera* (wide pan with long handle) with four spoonfuls of olive oil sauté the chopped onion on a low flame until it is transparent. Add the tomatoes and the chopped garlic. Cook for 15 more minutes.
3. Debone the chicken and rabbit and sauté it in the sauce base. Season it and cover with the meat stock. Add the laurel and *pebrella* (or thyme) and cook it all together for 10 more minutes.
4. Add the bread cut irregularly and cook another 15 minutes, making sure the bread is not overdone. The secret of the dish lies in finding the exact point of cooking so that the bread is soft and juicy and the stock is reduced and thick.

There are almost as many gazpachos as there are hunters. The variants are almost endless with all types of meat, traditionally game and poultry, wild herbs and seasonal wild mushrooms. You can add strips of red pepper and ham cubes. The *pebrella* (*Thymus piperilla*) is a wild herb typical of the mountains in the north of Alicante. In many recipes all the ingredients are sautéed together and the stock prepared in the same gazpachera pan.

tombet de corder amb caragols
tombet of lamb with snails

for 4 people

* 800 g of chopped lamb * 2 dozen snails * 1 onion * 1 tomato * 1 hard-boiled egg * a fistful of almonds * 3 cloves of garlic * 1 cup of white wine * 1 bunch of rosemary * 1 bunch of thyme * parsley * ½ teaspoon of paprika * saffron * pepper * salt

1. Season the pieces of lamb with a pinch of paprika, freshly ground black pepper and a chopped garlic clove and leave to macerate in the fridge for two hours so that they soak up the flavour.
2. Clean the snails with water and salt several times and place them to cook on a very low flame with abundant water with a bunch of rosemary and thyme. As soon as they begin to come out of their shells, raise the intensity of the flame so that the water boils immediately. Cook them for 45 minutes and drain.
3. Prepare a sauce base in the mortar crushing the almonds with the egg yolk, saffron, parsley and a garlic clove.
4. Sauté the onion in a ceramic casserole dish with two spoonfuls of oil until it is transparent. Add a chopped garlic clove, the peeled and chopped tomato and the pieces of lamb. Season, raise the intensity of the flame and stir often so that it does not stick. When the meat is browned, add the cup of wine and leave to reduce a few moments on a high flame. Then turn down the flame again and leave to cook on a very low flame.
5. When the meat is almost cooked, add the snails and the sauce base. Cook all together for a few minutes and serve.

The *tombet* is typical of the dry counties of the interior of es Castellón. You can prepare it with rabbit, kid, chicken or rabbit. Also popular are the *tombets* with broad beans, green beans and cauliflower. The *tombets* of Les Useres, Benassalt, L'Alcora, Atzeneta and Figueroles enjoy great fame.
The word *tombet* comes from the verb (tumble or turn) and refers to the gesture of moving the casserole dish to turn the ingredients and avoid them sticking from the cooking.

valencian_cuisine

04

216_*arnadí* of pumpkin and sweet potato
218_bavarian cream of *turrón* from xixona and chocolate
221_*flaons* of morella
222_friar's balls
224_*rossegons* or *carquinyolis*
227_figs *albardados*
228_*panquemado* bun with orange
230_*monjávena*
233_flat bread of castellón
234_celestial flat bread

recipes for desserts

valencian_cuisine

arnadí de carabassa i moniato
arnadí of pumpkin and sweet potato

for 12 people

* 800 g of peeled sweet potato * 1.7 kg of peeled pumpkin * 300 g of ground almond * 500 g of sugar * 4 egg yolks * 8 spoonfuls seedless raisins * peel of 2 grated lemons * 1 stick of cinnamon * 1 teaspoon of ground cinnamon * a pinch of black pepper * Marcona almonds and pine nuts for decoration

1. Peel the pumpkin and the sweet potatoes, chop them and place them in a pressure cooker half covered with water along with the cinnamon. Cook them for 30 minutes from the time you turn the valve. Leave to cool, remove the fibres from pumpkin and place it in a cloth bag or cotton. Leave it hanging for the night so that it drains all the liquid.

2. Then pass both ingredients through a food mill. Place the mixture in a casserole dish on a very low flame with the sugar, cinnamon and grated lemon peel, stirring constantly. Add the ground almond and cook 5 more minutes. Add the four beaten yolks and the raisins, previously soaked and dried, and mix.

3. Spread this mass in a large ceramic casserole dish or in several individual moulds and give them the form of a pyramid using a spatula.

4. Pre-heat the oven at 180° C. Decorate the whole surface of the *arnadí* sticking on pine nuts and almonds. Sprinkle the surface with a mixture of sugar and cinnamon. Bake it a 180° C for 5 minutes. Lower the temperature of the oven to 150° C and cook for 15 more minutes. Remove the *arnadí* from the oven and leave to cool before serving.

There are many variations of this typical Easter recipe. One important tip: the cloth bag (*coixinera*) must be washed with neutral soap so that the pumpkin does not absorb the flavour.

valencian_cuisine

bavaresa de torró de xixona i xocolata
bavarian cream of *torró* of xixona and chocolate

for 8 people

* 1 tablet of *turrón* of Xixona * 300 ml of whipping cream * 250 g of chocolate fondant
* 3 eggs + 3 yolks * 6 laminas of gelatine * 3 spoonfuls of sugar + 3 spoonfuls for the caramel

1. Leave to soak in two bowls with three gelatine laminas in each one. Whip the cream. Heat three spoonfuls of sugar on a low flame until obtaining a caramel and pour it into the bottom of a mould for Bavarian cream.

2. Nougat of Xixona mousse: break up the nougat and blend it in bowl with the three yokes. Drain three gelatines, chop them and melt them in a pot with three spoonfuls of hot water. Add them to the nougat purée and stir. Add half of the whipped cream, mix carefully with circular movements and pour this preparation into the caramelised mould.

3. Chocolate mousse: chop the chocolate, melt it in a bain-marie and remove it from the flame. Drain the remaining gelatines, chop them and melt them in a small pan with some spoonfuls of water hot. Add the chocolate and stir so that they are well mixed.

4. Separate the whites from the yolks of the three eggs. Whisk the whites with a whisker. Beat the yolks with three spoonfuls of sugar and mix them with the melted chocolate. Add the remaining whipped cream and also add the whisked egg whites with circular movements.

5. Pour the chocolate mousse over the nougat mousse and leave the mould to rest in the fridge for a minimum of 6 hours so that it sets.

The nougat of Xixona mousse is also delicious on its own. Once made, serve in small dessert cups and leave to set in the fridge.

flaons de morella
flaons of morella

for 15 *flaons*

<u>for the mass:</u> * 250 ml of sunflower oil * 1 dl of aniseed * 2 spoonfuls of muscatel * 60 g of sugar * 600 g of flour

<u>for the filling:</u> * 100 g of cottage cheese * 50 g of ground almond * 1 egg * 1 teaspoon of ground cinnamon * 60 g of sugar * 1 egg yolk for painting the *flaons* * sugar for sprinkling * cinnamon for sprinkling

1. Filling: break the egg and separate the yolk from the white. Whisk the white into a merengue. Pass the cottage cheese through a sieve so that it is runny. Mix it with the yolk and a pinch of cinnamon. Add the sugar and stir. Add the whisked egg white and put to one side.
2. For the mass: sieve the flour on a work surface and form a volcano. Fill the central hollow with the aniseed, the muscatel, oil and sugar. Work the mass until all the ingredients form a uniform whole. Form a ball, wrap it in clingfilm and leave to rest in the fridge for 30 minutes.
3. After this time, spread the mass using a rolling pin and cut it into circles of about 12 cm diameter using a pastry cutter.
4. Place a spoonful of the filling on one side of the circles, close them in the shape of a half moon and join the edges in the form of a plait.
5. Brush the *flaons* with yolk or beaten egg, sprinkle them with a mixture of sugar and cinnamon and bake them at 180° C for 15 minutes or until they are golden. Remove them from the oven and sprinkle them with more sugar and cinnamon if you want. Leave them to cool before serving.

This recipe of Arab origin is the most typical sweet of the beautiful town of Morella and its county. It is made with *brull* or cottage cheese, obtained after boiling and draining the whey from the preparation of the traditional cheeses of the area.

valencian_cuisine

pilotes de frare
friar's balls

for 12 balls

for the mass:

* 300 g of flour * 250 ml of milk * 100 ml of sunflower oil * 3 egg yolks * 1 grated lemon peel * 50 g of baker's yeast * 2 spoonfuls of sugar * sunflower oil

for the cake cream:

* 300 ml of milk * 3 yolks * 70 g of sugar * 20 g of corn flour * a piece of lemon peel * 1 teaspoon of vanilla-flavoured sugar

1. Dissolve the yeast in warm milk. Add the oil, yolks, sugar and grated lemon. Add the flour and knead until it forms a ball.

With moist hands, take the dough and form twelve balls, leave them to rise on a damp tea towel until the double in size.

2. For the cream: bring the milk to the boil with a piece of lemon peel. As soon as it boils, remove from the flame, cover and leave to cool. Beat the yolks with the sugar and the vanilla-flavoured sugar. Add the now warm milk stirring continually. Keep a little of the milk to dissolve the corn flour.

3. Heat the preparation on a very low flame. Add the corn flour and cook for a few minutes until the consistency is a thick cream. Remove from the flame and throw away the lemon peel. Leave to cool.

4. Fry the balls of dough in a pan with abundant hot sunflower oil until they brown (the oil should not be too hot so the balls brown too quickly and are raw inside). Drain them on absorbent paper and leave them to cool. Fill them with the cake-making cream, sprinkle with sugar and serve.

This delicious recipe, an authentic godly sin as its name indicates, is typical of the pastries of Castellón.
You can replace the sunflower oil with butter.
To make it easy to fill them, you can freeze them once fried and cold.

valencian_cuisine

rossegons o carquinyolis
rossegons or carquinyolis

* 350 g of flour * 200 g of raw unpeeled almonds * 200 g of sugar * 2 teaspoons of powdered yeast * 2 eggs + 1 yolk * ½ grated lemon peel

1. Beat the eggs with the sugar until it is foamy. Add the grated lemon and the yeast and mix. Add the flour gradually, stirring until obtaining a homogeneous mass.
2. Add the almonds, mix and several small bars of the same size, approximately 35 cm long and 5 cm wide.
3. Preheat the oven at 170 °C. Brush the bars with the beaten yolk with a spoonful of water and place them in an oven tray on slightly oiled baking paper. Bake them at 170° C for 20 minutes or until they have the sufficient consistency to be able to easily cut them.
4. Remove them from the oven, place them on a work surface and cut them crossways in slices of about 1.5 cm thickness.
5. Place the small slices on the oven tray again and bake them for another 10 minutes.

There are many recipes for this popular sweet. The secret is ensuring the mass does not have too much flour and to cut it half way through cooking, when it has not yet hardened. The final minutes of cooking will ensure they are toasted and crunchy.

figues albardades
figs *albardados*

* 500 g of dry figs * 350 g of flour (or the amount possible) * 15 g of compressed yeast * 1 cup of hot water * a pinch of salt * sugar for coating * olive oil for frying

1. Dilute the yeast in the hot water with a pinch of salt. Add the flour that it will take until obtaining a gelatinous paste, which is not thick. Cover and leave to ferment for 45 minutes until it begins to form bubbles.
2. Meanwhile, prepare the figs removing the stalk and open them at the centre in the form of a book.
3. Take the open figs two by two, pass them through the mass and fry them in a pan with hot oil until they are browned.
4. Leave them to drain on absorbent paper and sprinkle them with abundant sugar before serving.

To give them more flavour, the figs can be left to macerate in a spirit, such as brandy or muscatel.

valencian_cuisine

panquemao a la taronja
panquemado with orange

5 units

* 600 g of flour * 130 g of sugar * 25 g of baker's yeast * grated peel of 1 orange * 3 eggs + 1 egg for brushing * 40 ml of sunflower oil * 75 ml of milk * 25 ml of sweet aniseed * a pinch of salt

1. Dilute the yeast in warm milk. Sieve the flour in a large bowl, form a volcano and add the other ingredients. Knead until achieving a homogenous mass. Cover it with a tea towel and leave to ferment until it doubles in size.

2. Flatten the mass with your hands to remove all the gases. Then, with moist hands, take portions and form five balls of about 200 grams. Place them well separated on a baking tray lined with baking paper. Cover with a tea towel and leave to ferment for another 2½ hours.

3. Preheat the oven at 180° C. Using a very sharp knife, make a transversal cut in each of the balls. Brush them with the beaten egg and sprinkle them with abundant sugar soaked with a few drops of water. Bake in the middle of the oven at 180° C for 25 minutes. Leave them to cool on a grille before serving.

You can use orange juice instead of milk. This recipe, with its many variants, is very popular at Easter. When it has a hard-boiled egg in the middle it is known as the Easter *mona* cake. Very similar recipes have other names according to the area: *panou, tonya, cóc, fogassa, pa socarrat*… If the mass has nuts and raisins they are called *reganyaes*.

valencian_cuisine

almoixàvena
monjávena

for 8 people

* 4 eggs * 100 g of flour * 80 ml of olive oil * 240 ml of water * 1 spoonful of sugar * 1 teaspoon of lard * 1 teaspoon of ground cinnamon

1. Heat the water with the oil in a casserole dish and, on boiling, add the flour all at once. Remove from the flame and mix until obtaining a homogeneous mass that does not stick to the sides of the pot.
2. When the mass has cooled down, add the eggs one by one and stir for 10 minutes.
3. Preheat the oven at 230° C. Slightly grease a baking tray and place the mass on top so that it is thin, approximately 1 cm in thickness.
4. Spread over the mass some pats of butter, lightly sprinkle with sugar and cinnamon and bake at 200° C for about 30 minutes, until it has risen and browned.
5. Remove from the oven, leave to cool and sprinkle with more sugar and cinnamon before serving.

Typical of Ontiyent and Xàtiva, this recipe has different names such as *monchovenes*, *monjàvenes* or *monxavinas*. It is often eaten at Lent and All Saints Day as an accompaniment with coffee or as an afternoon snack. You can serve it with syrup, melted chocolate or honey and, if it has risen well, can be carefully opened and filled with a cream of condensed milk and yolk.

coca de castelló
flat bread of castellón

for 8 people

* 180 g of ground almond * 120 g of pumpkin fruit * 360 g of sugar * 540 g of potato * 4 eggs
* 1 sachet of blue soda or 1 powdered yeast * ½ grated lemon peel * a pinch of cinnamon

1. Preheat the oven at 170° C. Peel the potatoes and cook them in a casserole dish with boiling water for 30 minutes, draining them and passing them through the food mill. Mix the purée obtained with half the sugar.
2. Break the eggs and separate the yolks from the whites. Using a whisker whisk the egg whites into a merengue with the rest of the sugar.
3. Beat the yolks and mix them with the whisked whites. Add the ground almond, grated lemon peel, blue soda powder, grated pumpkin fruit and the potato purée.
4. Line an oven tray with baking paper and spread the mass over it. Bake it for 15 minutes at 170° C, lower the temperature to 120° C and continue cooking for 15-20 more minutes or until in pricking it with a needle, it comes out clean.
5. Leave the flat bread to cool and sprinkle with icing before serving.

This flat bread of humble origin is known popularly as *coca de creïlla* (potato coca of potato).

valencian_cuisine

coca celestial
celestial flat bread

for 8 people

* 300 g of ground almond * 300 g of sugar * 200 g of pumpkin fruit * 3 egg whites * 4 yolks
* walnuts, morello cherries and crystallised fruits for decoration * 1 wafer biscuit (*neula*)

1. Preheat the oven at 180° C. Grate the pumpkin fruit and mix it with the three yolks.
2. Whisk the egg whites with a whisker and then add the sugar and continue beating until obtaining a merengue. Add the ground almond and continue beating until it is all well mixed. Divide the mass into two parts.
3. Spread the first part of the mass carefully over a wafer and spread the pumpkin fruit preparation on top.
4. Cover with the rest of the mass and brush the surface with the remaining yolk. Decorate the flat bread to taste with rectangles of crystallised fruits, morello cherries and walnuts.
5. Bake at 180° C for 20 minutes making sure it does not burn. Leave to cool on a grille and serve.

This flat bread was very popular around Christmas in the villages of the north of Castellón. It is also made in some Valencian counties.

valencian_cuisine

glossary

All i pebre: traditional preparation based on garlic and paprika, thickened with bread or ground almonds. The most typical is prepared with eels from the Albufera lagoon.
Aladroc: anchovy (*Engraulis encrasicolus*).
Blat picat or forment picat: chopped wheat. Laborious traditional stew made with previously soaked wheat.
Bajoques: green beans. In some counties they are called *bajoques al pimiento* (the *bajoques* or *pimentons farcits*, stuffed peppers are very popular).
Borra: popular dish with cod or frigate mackerel (also with tuna or cuttlefish), potatoes, spinach, oil, dried peppers, garlics, paprika and salt. It is usually served with poached eggs. In the versions known as *borretas* they often have less ingredients.
Brull: cottage cheese.
Caragolada or caragolà: festive meal for social occasions made with snails.
Casca: circular sweet made with marzipan that can be filled with yolk, sweet potato or pumpkin. It was usually eaten on the day of the Magic Kings before the King's Day ring cake became more popular.
Cassoleta: small dish. It refers to the shape of the moulds used to shape the cheeses.
Creïlla: potato.
Crespells: general name that describes several types of sweets made in different counties.
Espencar: crumble, flake.
Fanguejat: mud dredging. Agricultural operation that consists of breaking up the land of the rice fields, previously flooded at a low level, using a dredger or cage attached behind the tractor in order to fertilise and seed.
Farinetes: pap.
Fartons: long sugared buns, covered with icing sugar, to accompany the tiger nut milk, *horchata*.
Figatells: oval-shaped meatballs made with mince lean pork, pig liver and kidney, aromatised with spices and wrapped in a membrane or trimming.

Flaons: cakes in the form of small pies that are filled with cottage cheese.
Garreta: black pudding, hock.
Llanda (or llauna): metallic recipient, low and flat for baking in the oven.
Marjal: in agriculture, field or plot cultivated with rice. Geologically it is defined as a marshland close to the sea.
Minxos: small flat breads of wheat and corn, generally lengthened. They may contain ground peanut.
Pebrella: thyme (*Thymus pyperella*). Aromatic herb.
Pebreres: peppers (also *paprikas, pebres, pebrots, bajoques*).
Pericana: typical Alicante mountain dish that is eaten in winter, generally for the olive harvest to test the quality of the oil.
Porquejà or matança: slaughter of the pig.
Sèquia: irrigation canal. In the case of the rice field, the irrigation canals flow radially towards the Albufera lagoon and receive all the surplus water that comes from the Xúquer and Túria rivers.
Salmorreta: Alicante sauce made with ñoras, garlic, parsley, vinegar and roast tomato.
Tombet: recipe typical of the mountainous county of Castellón. The ingredients are tossed with the gentle sway that is practiced on a pan with handles.
Txulles: chop.
Riu rau: rural construction with porches, typical of the Alicante's Marina Alta, the function of which was to protect the wattle on which the raisins were dried from damp and rain.
Vaquetes: mountain snails.

valencian_cuisine

bibliography

Canut, Enric; Monné, Toni: *Quesos y paisajes*. Ed. Udyat. Barcelona. 2008
Carceller, Alicia: *Menjar i viure a Morella*. Ed. Empúries. Barcelona 1991
Dacosta, Quique: *Arroces contemporáneos*. Montagud Editores. Barcelona. 2005
Domínguez, Martí: *Els nostres menjars*. Vicent García Editores. Valencia. 1979
Font i Bel, Àngels: *La cuina de Sant Mateu. Maestrat ahir, avui i sempre*. lacuinadesantmateu.cat. 2011
Luján, Néstor; Perucho, Joan: *El libro de la cocina española*. Ed. Danae. Barcelona. 1970
Llorca, Carlos; Ruiz, Ángeles: *Gastroguía de la Costa Blanca*. Patronato Provincial de Turismo de la Costa Blanca. Diputación de Alicante. Alicante, 1999
Llorca, Carlos; De Diego, Pau; Ruiz, Ángeles: *Vademécum de cocina de la Marina Baixa*. Agència Valenciana del Turisme. Valencia. 1997
Martínez, Manuel M.: *Historia de la gastronomía española*. Ed. Alianza. Madrid.1989.
Millo, Lorenzo: *Cocina Valenciana*. Ed. Everest. León. 1995
Piera, Emili: *La cocina valenciana*. Algar editorial. Alzira. 2002
Seijoo Alonso, Francisco G.: *Gastronomía de la provincia de Alicante*. Ed. Villa. Alicante. 1974
Seijoo Alonso, Francisco G.: *Gastronomía de la provincia de Valencia*. Ed. Villa. Alicante. 1977
Tortosa, Paco; Prósper, Pepa. *L'Albufera. Guia de descoberta del Parc Natural*. Publicacions de la Universitat de València. Valencia. 2007
Vázquez Montalbán, Manuel: *La cocina de los mediterráneos. Viaje por las cazuelas de Cataluña, Valencia y Baleares*. Ed. Zeta. Barcelona. 2002
Vergara, Antonio; VV.AA.: *Anuario de la cocina de la Comunitat Valenciana*. Editorial Prensa Valenciana.
Watson, Jeremy: *Vinos de España*. Montagud Editores. Barcelona. 2002

index of recipes

rice dishes	**128**
rice with parsnips and kidney beans	130
rice stock with rabbit, saffron milk caps and vegetables	132
ship's soup	135
dirty rice	136
black rice	138
baked rice	141
rice with crust	142
rice with seafood of alicante	144
rice *del senyoret*	147
paella valenciana	148
paella alicantina	150
paella castellonense	153
seafood paella	154
cod and cauliflower paella	156
starters	**158**
orange and cod salad	160
salted tuna, tomato, orange and black olive salad	162
esgarraet	165
espencat	166
mullador of *sangatxo*	168
pericana	171
stew of la plana	172
octopus broth	174
noodles	177
flat bread of *mullador*	178
flat breads *a the calfor*	180
borreta of frigate mackerel with spinach	183
giraboix	184
shrimps with swiss chard	186
musician's stew	189
stuffed peppers	190
broth	192
fish main courses	**194**
all i pebre of eels	196
blanquillo of monkfish	198
sea bass stew	201
cruet of conger eel and vegetables	202
llandeta of red mullet	204
octopus with cardoon leaves	207
meat main courses	**208**
figatells	208
gazpacho of rabbit and chicken	210
tombet of lamb with snails	213
desserts	**214**
arnadí of pumpkin and sweet potato	216
bavarian cream of nougat of xixona and chocolate	218
flaons of morella	221
friar's balls	222
rossegons or *carquinyolis*	224
figs *albardados*	227
panquemado with orange	280
monjávena	230
flat bread of castellón	233
celestial flat bread	234

acknowledgements

Pablo Martí of Veses, Reme Benavent, Dani Boix, Dolors Amat, Flavia Silva, Oriol Casanovas, Salsadella garmers and cooperative, Restaurante La Pepica, Jorge Llorach (www. alcachofabenicarlo.com), Coop. Agrícola "San Isidro" of Benicarló, Vicent Peris, Antonio Albiol ("San Pedro" Fishermens' Guild of Vinaroz), Miquel Vives (www.quesosdecati.com), Demetrio Ferrando and family (www.demetriotrufadebenassalt.es), José and Mª José (Mesón el Viscayo), Fishermen's Community of El Palmar (www.cpescadoreselpalmar.com), Primitivo Rovira e Hijos (www.turronesprimitivo.com), Moltto, Germà Alcayde (www.chufadevalencia.org), Horchatería Sequer lo blanch (www.sequerloblanch.com), Jose Alfonso Sierra D.O Vinos Utiel-Requena (www.utielrequena.org), Cristina Correoso, Bodegas Emilio Clemente (www.eclemente.es), José Luis Claramunt, Bodegas Vicente Gandia (www.vicentegandia.es), Primitivo Quiles (www.primitivoquiles.com), Carmelitano Bodegas y destilerías.